In MOMENTS *of* SILENCE

RAIN JOHNSON

In MOMENTS *of* SILENCE

the BRIDGE
CONNECTING
GOD *to* WOMAN;
SPIRIT *to* SPIRIT

Xulon Press

Xulon Press
2301 Lucien Way #415
Maitland, FL 32751
407.339.4217
www.xulonpress.com

Unless otherwise indicated, Scripture quotations taken from the King James Version (KJV)—*public domain.*

Scripture quotations taken from the Holy Bible, New International Version (NIV). Copyright © 1973, 1978, 1984, 2011 by Biblica, Inc.™. Used by permission. All rights reserved.

Paperback ISBN-13: 978-1-66286-132-1
Ebook ISBN-13: 978-1-66286-133-8

author bio

In Moments of Silence started out as a question that was held out to God. The answer came back in such a beautiful way that it became a book not just for Rain, but for all women. This book is for all who seek to know the truth of who they truly are to God and our purpose on the earth. It is Rain's hope that you too live out loud the life God designed for you and the life you carry within your triune being.

In her own journey, Rain Johnson grew up in the church and still struggled with understating her value, purpose, and importance to God. She came to realize that in order to move forward and grow, she had to get real with herself admitting she didn't completely know who she was or where she belonged in the world. While the world put up one image of woman, Rain knew in her heart there had to be more. That she was created for more. Rain embraced the promises of God and began to seek Him for herself in an uncharted way, which revealed the beauty she held to God, mankind, and creation. Rain now lives with a new and wonderful outlook on life with gratitude for life like never before.

In Moments of Silence reminds women that they hold everything needed to live a victorious, successful life. And that it begins with first acknowledging God and connecting your spirit with the Spirit of God to receive. Now is the time to understand and live life as God intended. And then pass it on.

contents

dedication

This book is dedicated to women of all ages, races, and nationalities. May your journey be filled with wisdom, understanding, and victory. I pray that your spiritual eyes be opened even the more to experience the life God truly designed for you. I come into agreement with you that every dream and talent you have will be used to the glory of God. That you will succeed and prosper as you pour back into the earth that which God has poured into you. As the Spirit guides you to your destiny, which I know is going to be beautiful, remember to live a life of gratitude taking time to enjoy the journey of life. After all, you are the embodiment and essence of life.

acknowledgments

Before writing this book, I described myself very differently. I didn't fully understand God's will or plans for me as a woman. It wasn't clear to me why God created woman after looking around at a world where I saw constant contradictions to what I felt inside should've been viewed as beautiful. This book has everything to do with the Holy Spirit, whom revealed the truth of my worth and value. At a time when I felt rejected and even forgotten... God was there to mend the broken pieces and remind me that I am loved. That I have purpose. But I had to change my focus. This is why I give God (Abba) all the praise, all the honor, and all the glory for revealing to me who I am so I can truly live.

Special thanks to my husband, Kennie, who is my biggest fan and supporter for always being there to encourage my dreams. Thank you for being a man of God.

To my children Shawn and Brianna, I thank God for trusting me to be your mom. We've stuck together through a lot. I'm so glad I've had the privilege of watching you grow and blossom into adults having your own relationship with God – I love you always.

To my family and circle of friends, I cannot say thank you enough for always being there extending love and walking with me through some of the hardest and best times in my life thus far. I appreciate you always being there to listen.

introduction

I saw women still being portrayed as a sex objects, subservient to man, and still finding much resistance in breaking glass ceilings. But I felt that we as women were no longer the image of an emotional unqualified counterpart unable to hold key positions. Was I right? I had so many questions for God. Questions like, "Why would you create me just to continue to live in a world where women would be sexually exploited, globally undereducated, unprotected, and denied equal economic opportunities?" There was this strong *purpose* feeling of purpose brewing inside of me bigger than I could've imagined. And so, began my search to what would lead to an awakening and revelation into who I really am. And who you really are. No matter where you are in the world, what color, or class you are... knowing your value, importance, and purpose from the One who created you is key to living.

I admit that I had no idea what the chapters would contain or how long this book would be. But I did know that this would be divinely inspired, and I was embarking on a journey toward truth. I had to surrender myself and rely on The Holy Spirit to guide and teach me. Wow, He did just that! There are so many "nuggets" of wisdom and encouragement. So, take time to read, digest, and ponder each chapter as we focus on the many layers that construct who you are from the beginning of creation, present, and the journey ahead. It's very important to understand who you are and the importance of having a spiritual foundation. God is a Spirit and we that worship him must worship him in spirit and in truth (John 4:24). Let's jump right in with these important truths... you have the authority, right, and permission to approach The Creator personally and individually with confidence and boldness. Within the spiritual realm is where you commune with God. Your ultimate nature is the life you take in and send out. And the quality of life you have depends on your capacity to grow and change, not just for self but for the world. As you continue to read you will find there is so much beauty and purpose to your life. You were made to experience life in its fullness beyond mere existence.

-free willed-

We are free-willed beings. And making our own choice is the ability to select from a number of options, ruling out and dismissing, and ultimately reaching a decision. So often we make a choice based off our wants and desires, but the right choice, the life changing choice, involves hearing and responding to God who holds the play book of life in His hands. Seems easy, right? But there is a cost to choosing to follow God's way. It involves seeing and esteeming not only self but others; caring about others. It's choosing to be healed from every internal infirmity that causes you to be unhealthy.It's confessing the truth of self-inflicted pain you've brought into your own life and forgiving yourself, releasing the pain, letting go of the heavy burdens you've carried, and forgiving others for any hurt they've caused. This opens the door to God's joy. It's humbling yourself and receiving healing. Being free-willed involves being freed to make good choices. You must seek the Lord who will keep you awake and give you the strength to resist ungodly impulses to go back into the unconscious ways of the world with all its deception(s). Being disconnected from God means there's a strong possibility that you'll select a choice not in His perfect will for you. God is our LIFE line. God's perfect will is for our good and for His glory (Rom. 8:28).

A conscious and deliberate decision reflects what you've chosen to be first in life. If you've chosen to place God first, you receive spiritual power which renews the mind. A renewed mind is a *power* sound mind that's healthy, able to render sober judgment, and self-controlled so that you can discern God's will which is flawless and complete (Rom. 12:2). The heart and intellect (thinking) are closely connected (Matt. 13:15) and function together in decision making. Whatsoever you think in your heart is what you are (Prov. 23:7). A choice is more than a mindless action, it's intertwined with your spirit, mind, and heart. Therefore, careful attention must be placed on the contents within the mind and heart because there your true nature/character is revealed. Finally, making good choices starts with strengthening the spiritual life.

Refusing to believe in God and not desiring to retain God in the mind is also a choice but this choice will more likely lead to fulfilling the desires of the flesh, not the spirit. In our humanity, we inherently seek something greater than ourselves. God brings you into harmony with His will. And the Spirit of God (Holy Spirit) guides your life revealing purpose (gifts, talents) placed in you for His glory. Every experience should be brought before God for clarity and direction. In the presence of God balance is found. Outside of this space are feelings that sway judgement toward wrong reactions and decisions. As women, our emotions serve as "sensors" that guide our expression and deepen our inward call and connection to God, Our Father and Creator.

> Only love is trustworthy. For we are commanded to love God with all of our heart (Mark 12:30) and with a pure heart (1 Tim. 1:5). Love will not fail.

～つ

-design layers-

God led me to applying art techniques to reveal His vision of how He designed woman and how truly loved we are. Art reflects an artist's attitude toward color as well as technique. They take in and incorporate influences that are then reworked into an inspired personal vision. Similar to art, God created woman with several layers producing a Work Of Art (WOA). Woman expresses the thoughts and views of The Creator. She is painted better than a Leonardo Da Vinci, Picasso, Gustav Klimt or Vincent Van Gogh could ever be. As you continue to read this book you will be able to: *Work of Art*

- Confirm woman as an original Work Of Art; not a reproduction.

- Reaffirm who created woman. Looking for God's signature and identifying marks. *The identity of the artist makes a large difference in the value of the work particularly if the artist is well known.

- Learn the provenance of woman and the history of her creation.

The Creator reflected His character in your innermost being with the colors, shapes, and textures He chose. God sees and knows beyond face value into the heart and spirit. Today is the day to come into the revelation of your true value. God promises, "But if from there you seek the LORD your God, you will find him if you seek him with all your heart and with all your soul." (Duet 4:29). Today, I'm no longer confused about who I am. I stand out and contribute to the world. My understanding of who I am has changed because now I know that I am God's WOA (Work Of Art). I am a receiver and I am a giver of life. I belong to the True and Living God who made me for His divine purpose; set apart for His glory. I am shaped and birthed with purpose, meaning, and destined for victory both now and beyond the grave. Yes, I am made in the image of God. And yes, I am God's woman.

> As women, we give and give but don't take time to receive.
> In fact, we are designed to receive. Life is filled with joy,
> love, security, and purpose. So, stop – be silent – receive
> from God.

Before you continue, let's be clear in understanding the threefold nature of God; three in one. He is God the Father, God the Son, and God the Holy Spirit; distinct yet one sharing essential sameness. In other words, they are simultaneously and eternally three in one. The trinity of God is considered a divine mystery, beyond our human comprehension, but reflected through scriptural revelation. And we, created in the image of God, are spirit, soul, and body. Each different but united as one. So, as I address mankind you'll understand it means we are an inferior triune being.

Work Of Art

A product of the fine arts; a painting or sculpture of high
artistic quality
Something giving high aesthetic satisfaction to the viewer or listener

Genesis 1:27-28, 2:18, 2:21-23

Verse 27 So God created man in his own image, in the
image of God created he him; male and female created
he them. 28 And God blessed them, and God said unto
them, Be fruitful, and multiply, and replenish the earth,
and subdue it: and have dominion over the fish of the sea,
and over the fowl of the air, and over every living thing that
moveth upon the earth.

Verse 18 And the Lord God said, It is not good that the
man should be alone; I will make him an help meet for him.

Verse 21 And the Lord God caused a deep sleep to fall upon
Adam, and he slept: and he took one of his ribs, and closed
up the flesh instead thereof; 22 And the rib, which the Lord
God had taken from man, made he a woman, and brought
her unto the man. 23 And Adam said, This is now bone of
my bones, and flesh of my flesh: she shall be called Woman,
because she was taken out of Man.

-one-

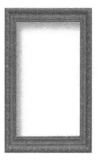

-silence-

woman
| **wom•an** |

an expression, like art, of God's creative skill and
thoughts. Woman made in the image of God is His
portrait, sculpture of beauty with emotional power
to be appreciated synonyms: work of art, fine art

-questions-

The questions I held out to God were..."Why did you create woman? Am I created to be subservient to man, a sex object, lesser than man? What's my purpose?" I simply put it all out there without being sure if or when I would a get a response. I waited, listening. My heart was open, and my mind was ready to understand the purpose and design for which I was created. Then I rested, knowing that I asked and it was now up to God. And guess what? Answers slowly started pouring in like ocean waves of thought, divine inspiration, and scripture. Answers beyond my limited scope of thinking were unfolding before me like a beautiful poem, resounding glorious song, and harmonic melody all opening and flooding my soul. In fact, the answers were so beautiful that I was compelled to write them down to share this spiritual encounter in this book because something this good should not be held onto but shared.

God's thoughts toward women are evident in every stroke of His creative brush onto the canvas of our design. Within every application of His perfect protective layer to our canvas there's purpose infused. Beautiful arrays of color that are composed of many interconnected parts appear as God applies layering to our life. Yes, everything about us works together for good, producing the amazing flawless Work Of Art (WOA) that we are. We are an acclaimed mas- terwork! Our nature, characteristics, and emotions *magnum Opus* all mark greatness. Far from one-dimensional, woman at every angle tells a story and expresses a truth. Her beautiful background and foreground images, like art, shape out adding well defined details to her place and reason for existence on the earth. Woman's beauty flows from the inside-out beyond the shape of her body or the opinions of others. And we, like art, are made to captivate and leave an everlasting impression amongst The Creator's vast Works Of Art. To truly grasp the magnum opus that we are, we must return to the core of who woman really is as defined by The Creator.

-silence (core)-

Visualize yourself standing before The Creator of the universe as a blank canvas in silence. There is no sound; no distractions. You're not yet filled with expression or direction; empty. Your mind is free and tranquil. In this moment you feel that you're exactly where you're supposed to be, carrying no weight, no burden, and no responsibility... you're mindfully present. Its right here that woman started with The Creator and it remains here as the starting place of producing a more effective you. It's in these moments when God performs His most marvelous works and miracles. Woman's first layer on her canvas is –

Silence Silence *Silence*. God directed me   *breathing*
towards the beginning of time revealing silence is
more than the absence of sound. Silence is an innate characteristic that we all have, much like breathing, connecting us to The Creator. It's the

path to encountering God; a place of renewal. Real beauty flows from the inside to the outside. For God is concerned about the heart and not outward appearance (1 Sam. 16:7). In Matthew 5:8 we are told that only the pure in heart shall see God. The heart is associated with activities of the mind, connected to feelings, and affections. By positioning our heart in submission to God we are acknowledging and surrendering to The Creator of the universe as His WOA. Silence can be so loud! Silence occupies the mind with God and all of His great spiritual truths. Truths like: God loves you with an unfailing love and has drawn you to Himself (Jer. 31:3). He died for you (John 3:16). God will never leave you or forsake you (Heb. 13:5). All things are possible with Him (Luke 1:37). God's faithfulness is one of His biggest characteristics (Deut. 7:9). And His forgiveness is perfect (Mic. 7:19).

Art is a process; woman is a process

Silence is worship involving your total self offering reverence, respect, and honor to God who created all things. And worship transcends and penetrates ordinary space, awakening you to the awareness of The Spirit's presence. This presence changes/shifts the atmosphere from "normal" to holy. You will see things differently in this space. Not with physical eyes but with spiritual eyes. Things you thought were important will become less important because God sheds a new light on what really matters. Other forms of worship include prayer, confession, and meditation. Silence, like exercise, needs to be practiced daily to sharpen our awareness to the divine presence of God. Our concentration should be on things that are true, honorable, just, pure, lovely, commendable - if anything is excellent or praiseworthy... think about such things (Phil. 4:8). God is worthy of all glory, honor, and power (Rev. 4:11). And in Colossians 3:2 we are instructed to set our affections on things above. Silence is where we commune, pour out chief concerns in life, listen for direction, and seek purpose. It's the place where we can recall the things that God has done for us. Note: silence is repetitious going over matters in the mind, and silence expresses appreciation and gratitude for the truth of who God says we are. Yielding to the Holy Spirit elevates your spirit and places the soul and body in their perspective order.

> Worship is your human response to the perceived divine presence of God. To properly acknowledge Him, you need to know that He is omniscient (all-knowing), omnipresent (present-everywhere), omnipotent (all-powerful), holy, sovereign, faithful, infinite, and good.

Reflection Moment: God's thoughts toward you are evident in every stroke of His creative brush into your design. In Solomon 4:7 we are told that we are altogether beautiful and there is no flaw in you. Do you see yourself as God does? If not, how can you begin?

-the beginning-

Genesis 1:1-3 In the beginning God created the heaven and the earth. And the earth was without form, and void; and darkness was upon the face of the deep. And the Spirit of God moved upon the face of the waters. And God said, let there be light: and there was light.

We can't go back further than "In the beginning". This verse tells of the earth being without purpose or light until The Spirit of God passed upon it. Note: when The Spirit of God moves, creation takes shape and emptiness is filled. The earth is seen as a resource but not the source of life. Life is found in The Spirit of God who provides *filled* clear definition and distinguished details, as in art, from beginning to end. There are no mistakes with God. Everything God creates has meaning, value, and importance. It's important to know that silence is often the posture of waiting for The Spirit of God to reveal Himself to us. And in the waiting allow the mind to rest where you will be kept from anxiety and within well-founded confidence... that is, if you choose to be kept. Our job is to seek the Kingdom of God above all else (Matt. 6:32-33) The Holy Spirit's job is to answer or lead you to the answer.

The book of Genesis is a book about beginnings.

First Day – Light (Gen 1:3-5)

Second Day – air spaces (firmament) (Gen 1:6-8)

Third Day – dry land appears and plant life (Gen 1:9-13)

Fourth Day – sun, moon, stars appear (Gen 1:14-19)

Fifth Day – animal life (biology) (Gen1:20-23)

Sixth Day – fertility of creation and creation of man (Gen 1:24-31)

Seventh Day – sabbath/rest (Gen 2:1-3)

Creation communes with God and through creation God is revealed. The universe, in majestic harmony, declares His mighty acts from the tiniest microscopic material displaying order and design to the largest mountain reaching upward towards the heavens. And though there is no speech or language heard, the vastness of the universe bears testimony to God as Creator (Ps. 19:1-4). Yes, all creation declares that God is organized! The heavens offer silent continual testimony of God just as all people, in every language, are able to understand God's revelation of Himself (non-verbal form) and have a clear awareness of Him. Note: revelation of God through nature does not equate to worshipping creation rather than The Creator. Beauty and wisdom God used in creating the earth is likewise revealed in us.

> God makes Himself known to creation revealing His will. God is seen through people, nature, the heavens, and universe. He desires fellowship with us and wants to uncover and disclose what was not previously known. We, made in His image and likeness, are a direct creation of God; reflection of God. Silence puts you in the right posture to receive.

Woman is included in the account and establishment of the earth, universe, and mankind

～

-access-

Silence is a one-on-one (private) connection with
private
The Creator restoring power, purpose, and renewing life
but in order to receive next steps we sometimes have to shut down/off
things that drain or distract us. Returning to silence ceases wandering
and quenches thirst as you're within the secured foundation of God.
Silence provides an atmosphere of security, relaxation, inspiration, and
replenishment. As women, we hold, nurture, and support mankind.
In order to do that effectively we have to tap into the pulse of God where

He is constantly calling us to His continued plan for creation. Silence is accessed through:

Meditation - turning the mind toward God and His spiritual truths, pondering upon it, and correlating it to our own life. While the wicked meditate upon violence, the righteous stand before God recalling His truths which are evident in the heavens, nature, and humanity.

> Hebrew (hagah) - "to utter in a low sound" denoting the growling of a lion or the cooing of a dove.

Meditation is repetition. It's going over a matter in your mind; constant recollection. In Philippians 4:8 we are instructed to think on the things of God; whatever is true, honorable, right, pure, lovely, good repute, all excellence, and things worthy of praise. Meditation is communing and being renewed, which can be done by reciting scripture, recalling past deeds, studying other lives in scripture, or focusing on life/purpose with gratefulness. It changes our attitude toward distractions and produces confidence in God. Meditation is important and pleases God.

Prayer is communicating thoughts, needs, and desires to God. Genuine prayer calls for moral and social accountability to coincide with it as you seek His will under His authority (Hos. 7:14). Through honest prayer you discern wrong, right, and glean wisdom. Proverbs 31:26 says, when she speaks her words are wise and she gives instructions with kindness. Prayers can ask pardon, seek communion, protection, deliverance, healing, and exoneration to name a few. We should have a regular and intense prayer life which can be aloud for the benefit of others, silent, or an intercession for others. Although prayer can be aloud, it should not be offered to impress others or long-winded in an attempt to manipulate God. We should not pray selfishly, with corrupted character, or with injured relationships. Prayer reflects our unity with The Creator and our desire to glorify Him. While God knows our needs, we still must ask. God desires to answer yet we must patiently persist. Prayer does not have to be eloquent, it just needs to come with faith. Prayer leads to a closer communion with God and a greater understanding of His will for our life. Postures of prayer can be kneeling, standing, eyes open, eyes closed, silently, aloud, in public, or in private. It's not the position of the body that matters but rather the attitude of the heart.

Your desire should be to stand blameless before God with a clear conscience. Take note that depravity is also said to issue from the heart. Scripture tells us that the heart is deceitful above all things and desperately wicked (Jer. 17:9). And within the heart comes *heart* defilement in evil thoughts, murder, adultery, fornication, theft, false witness, slander (Matt. 15:19). Always check the condition of your heart to see where God can do His good work(s) within you. For God's laws are written in your hearts and your conscience is proof of this (Rom. 2:15). You can be renewed in your heart (1 Sam. 10:9). And you must believe in your heart to be saved "for with the heart man believeth unto righteousness" (Rom. 10:10). Access involves love which is housed in the heart. It's such a strong emotion and completely opposite of hate. God commands you to love Him with all of your heart (Mark 12:30). The goal of this instruction is to keep a pure heart (1 Tim. 1:5). With continuous love for God and a position of uninterrupted silence, you remain ready for life. Do not allow wickedness to enter the heart (mind) condemning you before God.

Prayer corresponds to your understanding of who God is

God wants you to desire to know Him (Heb. 11:6). Desire to know who He really is and what He has to say concerning your life and all life. We can know and understand a lot about Him (1 John 5:20) and His character. Note: knowing facts about God is not the same as knowing God personally. A personal experience with God fills you with knowledge of His will through spiritual wisdom and understanding (Col. 1:9, 10). This filling comes by way of the Holy Spirit who helps us know the deeper things of God (1 Cor. 2:9, 10) distinguishing truth from error (1 John 2:27). The greatest experience in life is to know and understand God.

Reflection Moment: Whenever you feel unloved, unimportant, or insecure recall who you belong to (Eph. 2:19-22). List ways you can strengthen your spiritual connection.

-stillness-

Woman is designed for success. That's a simple yet powerful sentence. Owning this truth involves overcoming distractions and negative thinking in order to maintain a spiritual connection; mentally and emotionally. While silence renews inner peace, self-discovery, energy, creativity, mental clarity, and emotional well-being... it also provides the atmosphere for God's abundant life, which brings us to the next beautiful layer and spiritual revelation – **Stillness** Stillness *Stillness*. Stillness simply is silence on repeat. It's built momentum of reiterated silence that reinforces the spiritual *reiterated* connection while adding the ability to function or live day to day fulfilling your designed purpose. Stillness increases your ability to perceive and respond to the movement of the Holy Spirit and God's will. This is beyond just coping with life or existing. This is enjoying the blessings of being alive knowing that God is in control. Here you're receptive to God's love and increasingly mindful of behavior and actions that are wrong. Just imagine the kind of day you will have WITH GOD walking with you and constantly revealing Himself, providing His wisdom, and giving you understanding into the world He created. This continuous state of silence offers peace of mind knowing that your steps are being ordered by God who only has good in mind for you. Through the Spirit you can access God daily and receive the help you need (Heb. 4:14-16). Consistent stillness enables silence to be less likely interrupted.

Stillness is remaining in the presence of God while living

Stillness...silence on repeat, is not a new concept. God used repetition throughout the Bible delivering instructions. Repetition is the act of doing, saying, or writing something again; a repeated action. For example, you are instructed to pray about everything (Phil. 4:6), pray continually (1 Thess. 5:17), and be in constant prayer (Rom. 12:12). Prayer coincides with silence and stillness. Repetition in the Bible is often used to bring attention to an idea. For example, love is mentioned 310 times in King James Version (KJV). Repetition places emphasis on things chosen as significant letting you know when to pay special attention. Likewise, in this book you will find *significant* repetition on key messages. Note: The only things you want to avoid repeating is an offense to God.

Isaiah 55:8 says it so well "For my thoughts are not your thoughts, neither are your ways my ways," declares the Lord. Many times, we get angry with God's way because it's not the way we would've done things but if it were up to us, we would coast through life without any troubles at all which doesn't develop faith, character, or strength. And without faith it is impossible to please God (Heb. 11:6).

Stillness yields undistracted and unrestricted movement in harmony with God's Spirit where you gain victory over mental distress that divides the attention or prevents concentration. Stillness maintains silence during life's changes, growths, experiences, and activities.

14

Psalm 92:12 speaks of the righteous flourishing like the palm tree and growing. In order to develop and grow spiritually you should implement silence (worship) and stillness daily into life. Every woman needs this from the CEO to the Homemaker. Experiences in life can bend and twist you away from who you are really meant to be, taking you away from your intended path. Or at least making the journey harder than it has to be. We all have struggles. Most of us, especially as women, spend a lot of time caring for others but forget ourselves, which opens the gateway of unhappiness, unfulfillment, lack of self-esteem, lack of joy, etc. Stillness provides a private spiritual space where you can truly just be yourself. God accepts you just as you are. Vent to God all of your issues, concerns, and fears. Be in the moment without worrying about tomorrow and allow God's Spirit to nurture you for a change so you are able to nurture others. Consider this your refill station. Receive spiritual nourishment which feeds the spirit, like food nourishes the body. Stillness offers refuge in the sense that it keeps you from sinking into obscurity or falling prey to weakness. It destroys forces of confusion and conquers chaos.

Life is a spiritual existence transcending physical mortality

Stillness forms an uninterrupted "barrier" preserving the triune-being from easily being "shaken" by life's events or experiences. It's not the absence of life or movement but rather it's life in action. It's a peaceful and joyful place in the presence of God. Exodus 33:14 says, "My presence will go with you, and I will give you rest". And then John 14:26 says, "but the helper, the Holy Spirit, whom the Father will send in my name, he will teach you all things and bring to your remembrance all that I have said to you". Stillness secures your place in the presence of God by keeping your heart and mind focused on God. Continuous communion is achieved by praying often. Jesus prayed often (Luke 3:21, 5:16, 6:12, 9:18,28) and instructs the disciples to pray.

Reflection Moment: The Lord will fight for you, you only need to be still (Exod. 14:14). In what ways can you remain still in the midst of adversity?

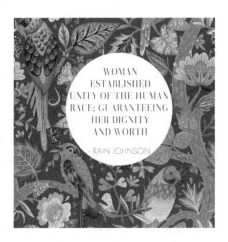

WOMAN
ESTABLISHED
UNITY OF THE HUMAN
RACE; GUARANTEEING
HER DIGNITY
AND WORTH

- RAIN JOHNSON

-barriers today-

Today, stillness is needed to be victorious over interruptions in a world of confusion. Interruptions are noise that work against your success and exist all around you. Confusion, discord, and interference all attempt to keep you from peaceful living and at bay from God, the source of strength. Noise attempts to block your signal and reception to silence. In today's world, noise can be a "first glance *noise* adjective" or description of a woman solely based on her physical qualities. Noise is in the confusion and senseless outcry of our girl's/woman's global lack of education, unprotected, and denied equal economic opportunities. Did you know that women often work more than men yet receive lower pay? Or that women and girls suffer the most poverty? This trending noise begins from conception to old age where girls and women experience gender discrimination; not limited only to countries where religion is law. Many rights are not recognized by law. This senseless sound is in countries where women are not able to own property or inherit land. There is social exclusion, honor killings, female genital mutilation, trafficking, restricted mobility, and early marriages. There is noise in women's denial to the right of healthcare, which increases illness and death. Gender equality furthers the cause of child survival and development for all society. Policies still need to be changed. If you can't identify it, noise can even be in how you see yourself when you are unable to fulfill responsibilities with ease. This affects the opinion of yourself and can carry over into other important aspects of your family, friendships, work, and overall health.

Woman is a beautiful portrait transcending birth, residence, occupation or nationality. She is not for others to interpret. God defines her.

Overlooked, excused, and denied. Noise attempts to keep you disconnected from true purpose. It seems like interference is constantly being thrown from every angle. It's found in the media, which encourages our young girls to lose the "little girl" persona by finding a way to display "stripper moves" or sexually suggested dancing as a way to prove womanhood. Maturity is becoming the push proving innocence is gone. Is this the type of message we want sent to our girls? How poisoned, corrupted, and deaf have we really become to the noise of sexual images and music lyrics? Our girls are being encouraged to put down baby dolls and pick up tween directed magazines. Magazines attracting our young under aged girls, who are still developing, with articles titled "21 mind blowing sex moves" or "265 hot looks & sexy hair secrets." Or maybe an article on "best birth control tips ever and things you should ask your Gyno". We cannot accept these misguided attitudes towards our girls, especially when we know these are not God's thoughts toward us.

> The Holy Spirit offers us knowledge by experience and knowledge by intuition. We can know by the anointing of The Holy Spirit. Intuitive knowledge is perceived from The Spirit without rational thought. Women draw from the intuition, keen emotions, and innate senses that God has placed in our instinctual design. Living by the spirit gives us insight and understanding into the world and people that we would otherwise not have.

There has been so much physical and psychological abuse that the spiritual connection can often get blurred by pain. Psychological abuse, often overlooked, is unlike physical abuse in that it leaves no obvious marks. However, regardless of the form abuse is manifested in, the purpose is the same... to dominate and control the other person creating emotions of fear, guilt, shame, and intimidation. The goal is to wear you down to keep you "in check." This not only destroys self-worth but causes anxiety and depression causing you to feel alone. Abuse and pain can cause you to become callus and hardened to inherent emotions and characteristics. The good news is that abuse doesn't have to penetrate the spirit. Noise can be silenced. Get rid of mind pollution and realize you are God's woman. Your life confirms that you have purpose. The horrible choice of another person forced on you is not the life experience(s) God intends for you. Silence and stillness will take you back to the road of your destiny and mute the noise. You can grow from every experience without remaining stagnant or nursing your wounds. There is a greater plan… if you choose to accept it.

Choices reflect not only your understanding of who you are, but who God is to you. Therefore, as a blank canvas embrace that you are wonderfully and fearfully made in the image of God (Ps. 139:14). The path to true authentic power and purpose involves seeking God who wants to be found. Yes, God wants to be intimately involved in every experience you have as He calls you to obey and believe in Him. Silence is a spiritual posture before God that regulates your triune being. It increases your ability to make good choices and leads you to understand God's will for your life.

> *Woman is purposed by God to fulfill a*
> *preordained role on this earth*

Barriers to God are:

Sin – actions rebelling against God and surrendering to the power of the forces against God; missing His purpose for your life. Sin hidden in your heart (resentment/bitterness) keeps you from truly experiencing living. Don't allow sin to harden your heart and lead you away from The Creator.

Fear – *human side:* expectation of imminent danger or disaster.

*Note: the fear you should have from *God side*: awe and reverence toward Him. This is the only fear we are to have. Those who fear God are blessed (Ps. 111:5) and enjoy God's goodness (Ps. 34:9).

Omitting silence (worship) – being too busy to connect to God will certainly keep you from hearing Him. Often times we disconnect ourselves from God thinking we know what's best. God wants to speak to us. Spend time in silence, prayer, scripture, and meditation to hear from The Creator.

We have the capacity to receive God's revelation
Of Himself & His will directly

By keeping the spirit woman first, you reestablish the order that was reversed at the downfall and actions of humanity *reestablish* rebelling against God. That downfall put the body first, soul, and then spirit. You don't want the body to lead because it leads by raw, unfiltered impulse, desires, and temptations while the spirit leads by The Creator's plan, will, and purpose connecting you in harmony to the true beauty of life, power, and purpose; operating and functioning as intended. Stillness renews you spiritually and requires a consistent walk that aligns you with God. Yes, you fall down and make mistakes... that's not the issue. No one is perfect. The issue is willfully and purposefully making mistakes, refusing to stop falling down. With God all things are possible (Matt. 19:26). You will not be tempted beyond your ability; God provides the way of escape (I Cor. 10:13). And Jesus is constantly interceding for you (Heb. 7:25, Rom. 8:34). God promised that He will never leave you nor forsake you, therefore, stillness can continue wherever you are. There is no mountain too high or valley too low where God cannot find you. God is there! Keep your heart in an attitude of worship. And live in The Spirit!

-gratefulness-

Being grateful is connected to worship. Gratefulness is your response to God for all that He's done and all that He is. We thank Him for His enduring love (Ps. 136:3), His goodness (Ps. 118:29), His everlasting mercy (Ps. 100:5), and for giving us life. For every good and perfect gift comes from above (James 1:17). Gratefulness reminds you of how much you have rather than what you do not have. When you focus on your blessings it keeps your heart and mind directed toward God. When I started to be thankful for things I often took for granted, like life, my perspective changed, and I became happier. Gratefulness helps you remember that God woke you up this morning and that it is He who fills your lungs with the breath (spirit) of life. You are told to give thanks in everything (1 Thess. 5:18). And if God allowed it, even though you may not understand it, find a way to be grateful for it. Again, choosing gratefulness is choosing worship. It's choosing silence.

Gratefulness ties into trust. And trusting God implies that you know all things work for the good and that nothing happens without God's consent and will. It's understanding that God is perfect, knows all things, and loves you. This confidence is not based on anything other than spiritual revelation and inward truth. It's believing God even though "the fig tree does not bud and confidence *confidence* there are no grapes on the vines" (Hab. 3:17). It's having confidence that God is with you, and He will bless you. However, ingratitude is being ungrateful and comes from a sense of entitlement. This is when arrogance and self-centeredness creep in and you begin to believe that everything you have has been achieved by your own doing. Or that you deserve good things apart from anything you've done or that you deserve better/more. Taking God's blessings for granted easily leads to callousness. Therfore, ask God to open your heart and spiritual eyes to see His goodness. His goodness is the source to sustaining spiritual life, natural life, good health, nourishment, and livelihood. Yes, life is truly a gift from God.

A desire to understand the truth about God yields understanding the truth about self

God reveals Himself directly and personally through miracles, covenants, and Jesus Christ. The Word became flesh (John 1:1, 1:14) so you can have a personal relationship with God and be led into His presence.

Reflection Moment: God is good (Ps. 136:1). List a few things you are grateful for.

-prayer-

Prayer involves self-examination and soul searching. It's where you examine your spiritual state, mental state, conduct, motives, etc. Prayer combats spiritual deception you encounter in the world. It involves reflection, meditation, and soul searching all rolled up into one. Prayer is about building a loving bond/relationship with The Father. Your prayer life should be occurring all the time throughout the day. In fact, you are instructed to pray without ceasing (1 Thess. 5:17). Your heart should be open to receiving from God as He pours into your being. Prayer is an opportunity to talk to God about everything/anything and receive instruction. Psalms 46:10 says, "Be still, and know that I am God: I will be exalted among the heathen, I will be exalted in the earth." The command to "be still" means to be weak, to let go, to release. Translated, this means to "cause yourselves to let go" or "become weak" in order to "know" that God is in control. Your prayers should be intense, as life is intense, and regular. Prayer is a means to surrender to God. It's often referred to as "dying to self." Following the command to pray enables you to know the saving power of God. This power is no longer trusting in self but rather trusting in His plan. Trust frees you from fear and offers you the peace of knowing that God is with and within you.

Prayer proclaims praise, asks pardon, and seeks communion, protection, vindication, and healing. Prayer unifies you with the Holy Spirit and guides you in your desire to give God glory. Prayer is your persistence to seek the will of God while remaining submissive to His authority. It's crucial that you pray! However, prayers are hindered by corrupted character (James 4:7) injured relationships (Matt. 5:23-24) or when prayer stems from selfish motives (James 4:2-3). Is every prayer answered? No. There are many examples in the Bible when deliverance was asked for yet did not come in the way expected. However, comfort was still found in God's sufficient grace. Learn to embrace the communion with God more than an answered request. Prayer makes a difference, if not in others... then in you.

Finally, BE FULL OF LIFE which is the very essence and core of what woman represents. Embrace, acknowledge, enjoy, and welcome the full presence, breath, and love of God residing in you. This is life. Don't lose sight of the truth that you are created to live. In everything you set out to do, look for God and His guidance. Remain in His presence and love. Seek first His kingdom and His righteousness and all these things will be given to you. Whether you eat or drink or whatever you do, do it all for the glory of God (Cor. 10:31). And don't worry about tomorrow, tomorrow will worry about itself (Matt. 6:31-34). God already knows what you need. Therefore, be anxious for nothing but in all things by prayer and petition with thanksgiving let your request be made known to God and the peace of God which surpasses all understanding will guard your hearts and minds (Phil. 4:6-7).

-two-

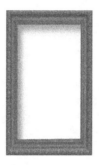

-purpose-

purpose

| **pur•pose** |

the desired goal for woman; Creators plan;
determination; to set as a goal for oneself
synonyms: design, function

There was a Samaritan woman at the well in John 4:4 who encountered Jesus as she went to draw water. I like this scripture because again you find a woman's one-on-one encounter with Jesus. And Jesus asked her, "Will you give me a drink?" This woman had no idea as to who was asking her for a drink at first, especially during a time when Jews did not associate with Samaritans. So, she questioned why He would ask her for a drink. In which Jesus answered, "If you knew the gift of God and who it is that asks you for a drink, you would have asked him and he would have given you living water." And Jesus went on to explain that the water she came to draw is not the living water He's offering her. He was offering water that quenches thirst and becomes a spring of water welling up to eternal life. And *living water* although Jesus knew and told her all that she had done, it didn't stop this encounter. Note: this woman was not the most righteous, in fact she had a bad reputation and had been married 5 times while currently living with a man also not her husband. The Samaritan woman recognized she was in the presence of more than just a man.

> Jesus told the Samaritan woman that true worshipers will worship the Father in the Spirit and in truth, for they are the kind of worshipers the Father seeks. Note: First Jesus explained His purpose and value in order to reveal to her, her true purpose and value. The same applies to you today.

When the Samaritan woman became aware Jesus was the Messiah she ran back to tell everyone what happened and many Samaritans believed because of her testimony. Note: Jesus waited for this woman at the well and permitted her *testimony* to be the first to declare He was the awaited Messiah. This encounter was life changing! Experiencing the presence of God is something that you can't keep to yourself because you want everyone to know and experience the love and acceptance you felt. Jesus not only spoke life into this woman, but He also reminded her of who she is; her value and worth. Today, we are being reminded of who we are.

Now, I thought about the importance of water to the Samaritan woman in this encounter. Water is necessary for the body, as God is necessary for life. Water in the body is needed by each cell to work, as God is needed within each part of our triune being in order to truly live. Finally, water in its pure state hydrates the body, but in an impure state water can harm the body. Likewise, it's that it's important to know the source from which you draw from because the source will either give life or take life away. God, the giver of life, is The Pure Living Water where we can draw from and receive perfect fulfillment from every craving of the world (fear, anxiety, greed, lust, etc.) God empowers and enables all who believe in Him to overcome. James 4:8 says, "Draw nigh to God, and he will draw nigh to you. Cleanse your hands, ye sinners, and purify your hearts, ye double minded." God will show you things in your life that need to be dealt with so you can have a pure heart. Run into the presence of The One who sees beyond faults and stop functioning outside of the realm of purpose.

God reveals Himself in 1) creation, purpose
2) restoration and 3) reestablishment

-weeding-

Sin needs to be plucked away. Like weeds in a garden, sin hinders growth and maturity. Weeding sin removes those things that keep us disconnected. This doesn't guarantee a pain free life, but it means you're a step closer to knowing peace that surpasses all understanding. When you do those things that honor God He will remain united with you in one spirit leaving no room for weeds. You are commanded to keep your body as a temple of the Holy Spirit who dwells in you (1 Cor. 6:19). In John 15:1-2 Jesus says, "I am the true vine, and my Father is the gardener. He cuts off every branch in me that bears no fruit, while every branch that does bear fruit he prunes[a] so that it will be even more fruitful." Be aware of temptations that try to hinder you from your purpose. Many times, it's in what you already know about God that the enemy will use to test/tempt you to include God's thoughts toward you. Note: Eve's temptation as she encountered temptation in the garden when satan caused her to question the instructions God gave.

God affirms your identity

You are chosen and complete. You are sealed with the Holy Spirit of promise (Eph. 1:13). God plans to prosper you not to harm you, plans to give you hope and a future (Jer. 29:11). God loves you and chose you (1 Thess. 1:4). And because God chose you, you are holy and beloved (Col. 3:12). It was God's mercy and love that made you alive with Christ (Eph. 2:4-5). You are worthy (Zeph. 3:17). You have access to God through faith in Christ (Eph. 3:12). You were brought near to God by the blood of Christ (Eph. 2:13). You have been raised up with Christ (Col. 3:1). You are complete in Christ (Col. 2:10). You are a member of Christ's body and partaker of His promise (Eph. 3:6). God will supply all your needs (Phil. 4:19). And His peace will guard your heart and mind (Phil. 4:7). You were once in darkness but now in the light of the Lord (Eph. 5:8). And your new self is righteous and holy in God (Eph. 4:24). You are God's workmanship created to produce good works (Eph. 2:10).

~~~>

-divine foresight-

You are always under God's careful watch. God's divine foresight sees the natural world, creation, the affairs of humankind, and each individual. Nothing escapes God. He directs the seasons (Ps. 104:19), clouds and winds (Ps. 104:3), stills the storms and encloses the mountain (Ps. 107:29; Ps. 65:6). You can be confident that God will direct you towards your call on the earth. God has an excellent track record of taking great care of creation and mankind! Let your spiritual walk be one that constantly looks for His wisdom concerning the universe, nature, and the affairs of *track record* mankind. Your Heavenly Father cares much more for you than the birds of the air or the lilies of the field (Matt. 6:25-34). Again, this doesn't mean that you are exempt from troubles but you are assured that God will be present with you in the midst of troubles. That's wonderful news! God is always working things for the good of those who love Him and have been called according to his purpose (Rom. 8:28).

Before making a future plan or future course of action be sure that you have the help of God. Make it a point to seek Him prior. Let your desire be that everything you do pleases God. God is soverign, in control, and all powerful. His influence and direction are extremely important to the outcome of your plans and life. Remember, your help comes from God the creator of heaven and earth. It's better to have a little with righteousness than great gain with injustice. While your heart plans your course, the Lord determines your steps (Prov. 16:8-9).

Reflection Moment: You are loved more than you know (Rom. 5:6). How can you live each day to the fullest with this knowledge?

~~つ

-walking together-

Let's look at Genesis 2:7 which says, "And the Lord God formed man of the dust of the ground, and breathed into his nostrils the breath of life; and man became a living soul." Then in Genesis 1:26-27 you are told that God said, "Let us make mankind in our image, in our likeness, so that they may rule over the fish in the sea and the birds in the sky, over the livestock and all the wild animals,[a] and over all the creatures that move along the ground." So, God created man in his own image, in the image of God created he him; male and female created he them."

God formed both man and woman securing their foundation and place in the earth. And both were made to fulfill God's preordained purpose on the earth set apart and above all other creation. Being made in the image and likeness of your triune God, who is Father, Son, and Spirit, means you are an inferior *preordained* trinity being spirit, soul, and body. With that being said, you as woman, have the right to live and walk in confidence knowing that you are God's

34

beautiful Work Of Art. All prior creation was spoken into being except for mankind who was formed from the dust of the ground. Dust being the most basic organic element associated with humility having little worth yet the element chosen by God. This element is also what humanity will return to upon death (Gen. 3:19). God here choose to form man differently from prior creation. Just as a potter forming a clay vessel, God shaped man giving humanity a place of prominence over the rest of creation (Ps. 8:5-8) creating humanity a little lower than the angels. Note: human lowliness in relationship with creation is expressed in the making of us from dust. It's the breath of life that made us a living soul (Gen. 2:7).

Breath (Hebrew – ruach) imitates the very sound of breath; same word for Spirit as is the case in both ancient Greek (pneuma) and Latin (spiritus).

God put His breath, His Spirit, within us & we became a living being with a soul, mind, heart, appetite, desire, emotion, and passion.

Genesis 2:8 "And the Lord God planted a garden eastward in Eden; and there he put the man whom he had formed."

God provided a garden where nourishment, both physically and spiritually, were received. Note: today silence is the *nourishment* environment where God provides nourishment both spiritually and physically. And within the garden God gave all that was needed to live, grow, and be productive. This perfect environment with perfect conditions is where God communed and met with both man and woman. It was theirs to dress and keep it as caretakers (Gen 2:15). "To keep" means to guard, protect, attend to. Today, God continues to give us dominion over the earth to care for it; not destroy it. And when you put your spirit first there's a natural beautiful communion and fellowship with God where you become alive, refreshed, and consciously aware of His presence. God's presence allows you to begin the process of being triumphant over attacks of the mind (fear, anxiety, depression, etc.) and body (caring for your body). However, if the body is placed first it will rule desires of the flesh and mind. You are told in 1 Corinthians 2:14 that the person without the Spirit does not accept the things that come from the Spirit of God but considers them foolishness, and cannot understand them because they are discerned only through the Spirit.

> The fellowship and communion God had with mankind in the beginning was in the perfect place and conditions. And the voice of God could be heard as He walked in the garden in the cool of the day. It was a garden where God placed mankind entrusting them to cultivate and keep it. And it was a garden where mankind sinned against God.

Allow what was in the beginning to also remain in you

Genesis 2:18 "And the Lord God said, It is not good that the man should be alone; I will make him an help meet for him."

Let's recap. Man was 1) formed from the dust of the ground 2) connected to the earth 3) established in relationship with God. And all creation was operating in harmony... yet man found himself without a companion and without help. While it's not revealed if God allowed man to come to this realization on his own or not, we do know that God determined who would complete him. God designated man with the help-meet woman. Note: "help meet" is a helper suitable for man as his partner and companion. It does not suggest subordination, sex object, servant, unequal counterpart, nor ownership. "Meet" emphasizes woman can be truly one with man enjoying full fellowship and partnership in the task God has given us.

> Man's role was to name all the wild animals & birds brought to him. He dressed the garden and kept it; till the ground, keeping the commandment to eat of every tree of the garden except of one.

Reflection Moment: Psalm 46:5 says, God is with her she will not fall. How can you take this promise and apply it to your life?

- *silence and woman*-

In Genesis 2:21,22 the scripture says "So the Lord God caused the man to fall into a deep sleep and while he was sleeping, he took one of the man's ribs and then closed up the place with flesh. Then the Lord God made a woman from the rib he had taken out of the man, and he brought her to the man."

God did something different and life changing here in creation. If you don't get anything else out of this book, this is what I want you understand... while man was in a state of sleep or worship, you find a moment in time (time as you know) where God and woman are alone together in creation. Remember, the earth and *alone together* creation are all operating within its role and purpose. And man is placed in a deep sleep preventing him from seeing the prophetic vision/revelation yet to come by The Creator. Stay with me. Because right here I pondered...why? Why would The All-Powerful, All Knowing, and All Mighty God chose to put man into a state of sleep. And to this question, The Holy Spirit revealed that this is the *moment of silence* woman first held with God. Here she received quality time, attention, and care, as previously granted to man. Life changing! This moment of silence that woman personally had with God missioned her into purpose. God demonstrated no superiority between man and woman during creation. And only after she spent quality time alone with The Creator in creation was she then revealed to man. Woman is the vessel God used to further make Himself known in a fully operating world. Woman bridged the gap between God and His creation. Being formed around existing life made woman the natural product of pre-existing creation (man) which helped her merge into an occupied moving world without skipping a beat. Life contains movement and progress. Take note that you are made to remain around life in order to continue movement forward in this world.

Woman received the same welcome package as man:

- got to know the voice of God
- fellowship and communion (walking & talking with God)
- acquainted with prior creation and given dominion over the earth and its creatures
- understood God's will; apart from man and with man

Your relationship with God is sealed. Jeremiah 1:5 says, that before He formed you in the womb He knew you. Note: without form (body) you are spirit. It's when you took on form, being born, is the beginning to relearning to put the spirit first. Communing with God confirms your capability, ability, intelligence, and qualification to approach God as His. Deuteronomy 31:8 says, "The Lord himself goes before you and will be with you; he will never leave you nor forsake you. Do not be afraid; do not be discouraged." God always desires to be Our Father who will protect, shape, and build you up. He wants to *impart* elevate, protect, and impart wisdom to you. Pursue God. Live life successfully, healthy, and confident. You are not made to merely exist. You are made to take the gift of life and expound upon it bringing forth new life. Note: being "built" from life also says you are made to be built up and not torn down. God desires that you increase and grow upon the foundation He provided. The New Testament demonstrates the rebuilding of woman back into her rightful place. Yes, God has empowered you under His authority and approval.

Get to know the voice of God. John 10:27 says "My sheep listen to my voice; I know them, and they follow me."

God speaks to us today through:

1) Scripture – The Bible holds the commandments you are to adhere to and is the tool used on all matters of faith & practice
2) Prayer – communication with God
3) Confirmation from Others – when God speaks to you; His word will be confirmed by others

A relationship with The Creator provides peace that will rule in your hearts when you seek His will (Col. 3:15)

The chief emotional attribute of God is love

Genesis 2:21,22 does not provide the dialogue between God and woman. But you do know woman was tasked with supporting and assisting, working alongside, man caring for creation. And in order to perform these duties woman had to be equipped with the necessary skill set to meet the needs of creation. This includes being sensitive, detail oriented, and capable of adapting to new situations quickly just to name a few. There's an expression that a man can build a house, but a woman makes it a home. Meaning, a woman can take what is given to her and make it grow/expand. You are capable of dealing with a situation and meeting difficulties. You fill the void in man and creation; filling in areas where man is not built to produce. And this is not just limited to offspring but any area that is fruitless or unproductive; empty. Focus on your God given skills to better adapt to any fast-paced situation. God will restore what you are constantly pouring out. But remember that the earth and all within it are a resource, but not the source of life. You can have all the resources the earth can provide but without The Source you will remain thirsty always seeking more. Maintain your relationship with God.

Note: man took no part or say in woman's creation. God takes all credit as her Creator. And God claims all rights to her establishment, formation, foundation, genesis, and imagination. Being formed and shaped "around existing life" is a beautiful symbol of how woman contributes to an already moving life; joining-in, adding value to, and bringing to completion.

Genesis 2:23 Adam says, "...This is now bone of my bones, and flesh of my flesh: she shall be called Woman, because she was taken out of Man".

God designated woman's role and determined by His own authority her purpose in agreement with Himself; Father, Son, and Holy Spirit. Then He presented woman to the man and man knew that woman was a part of him. And as with all prior creation, man named her...woman. Note: the name woman distinguishes us on the earth from other living things. Eve is the personal name, meaning mother of all the living (Gen. 3:20). By woman receiving the rib of man, it instantly connected them in a deep bond. A bond establishing their ability to work together side by side. Again, woman encountered God on a completed in-progress earth. She purposely was placed in a situation where all the moving parts and elements were in progress but still needed the support and nurturing piece she could offer. Woman, the nurturing piece, supported and helped to develop life. Note: in the corporate business environment women stimulate activity and growth through nurturing.

> The Hebrew word rib is translated - tsela used more than thirty times in the Old Testament and only translated rib in this passage referring to the side of Adam. The Sumerian word rib also means life.
>
> Woman being formed/created around the rib of man symbolizes her ability to grow (mature) where life exist. Now the opposite of that, is that our growth is stunted where life does not exist. Spiritually, we need to pursue God (who is life) so we can continue to mature.

Reflection Moment: We supply information that includes data/details to accomplish any task. What contributions do you see that we've made to support and compliment mankind?

-receive-

Receiving is a beautiful part of woman. You received life from God. And physically you are constructed to receive from man, conceive, and bring forth new life. Applying this same concept to your spiritual side, you'll see that the womb serves as an interior place for The Word of God (life) to develop and mature. The womb serves as the innermost part of your soul, the heart (as the seat of thought), choice, and feelings. Receiving The Word of God is a gift. And all who have received Him, those who believe in His name, have been given the right to be God's child (John 1:12). Receiving draws out your capabilities and possibilities to their full potential. The Samaritan woman, discussed earlier, was not the same woman after receiving The Word of God and releasing it back to mankind through her testimony. When the posture of your heart is right...you spiritually grow, which then leads to a more consistent life-style; maturity. No one is barren when it comes to receiving from God.

Mary, the mother of Jesus, conceived and received Jesus through the Holy Spirit while still a virgin. Mary represented goodness and profound commitment to the ways of God. God was able to use Mary as a vessel, but she had to receive the gift. And you too must receive the gift that God has for you. While the Holy Spirit lives inside every believer, it's only effective when you answer the call of God drawing us closer. Finally, Mary confirmed the human nature of Jesus Christ and the fact that we must receive from the Holy Spirit to *effective* be effective in the earth.

According to John 3:1-7, it is just as necessary to be born of the Spirit as it is to be born of a woman. For God is a Spirit. And His Spirit can be heard in the heart, mind, or even audibly to those who seek Him. God approaches us in the way He knows we will best receive. Jeremiah 1:5 "Before I formed you in the womb I knew you, And before you were born I consecrated you; I have appointed you a prophet to the nations."

Woman embodies the essence of life

Faith often takes you through experiences that require spiritual eyes instead of physical eyes. Romans 8:13 says, "For if you are living according to the [impulses of the] flesh, you are going to die. But if [you are living] by the [power of the Holy] Spirit you are habitually putting to death the sinful deeds of the body, you will [really] live forever." Receiving the power of the Holy Spirit is admitting the need for God in your life. This admission enables you to become approachable, ready, responsive, open-minded, sensitive, and sympathetic to mankind and creation. Now, receiving is not easy because there's also a constant battle against sin that often times tries to creep in. Job 23:10 says, "But he knows the way that I take; when he has tested me, I will come forth as gold." But adversity becomes easier when you choose to see God in everything recognizing He is in control. Developing this lifestyle is one of worship (stillness) which is key to not only hear God but act accordingly which allows purpose to freely flow. We're so programmed to seeing, touching, and feeling in the physical realm that we don't use our spiritual sensory skills. Luke 8:14-15 says, "The seed that fell among thorns stands for those who hear, but as they go on their way they are choked by life's worries, riches and pleasures, and they do not mature. But the seed on good soil stands for those with a noble and good heart, who hear the word, retain it, and by persevering produce a crop." Good soil is found in God. Receiving simply starts with believing in God's word.

> The fruits of the spirit are love, joy, peace, patience, kindness, goodness, faithfulness, gentleness, and self-control.

Philippians 1:6 "Being confident of this very thing,
that he which hath begun a good work in
you will perform it until the day of Jesus Christ."

There's a principle to receiving found in Mark 11:24 that says whatever you ask for in prayer, believe that you have received it and it will be yours. In other words, have confidence (believe) in the truth that you have taken into possession (received) what you have prayed for when you pray. Confidence is knowing that from that moment forward the miracle has been set into motion and that the answer is on the way. Faith is the certainty that your request has been heard and is as good as done. Faith is understanding the prayer and answer cannot be in heaven at the same time. Will you see immediate results? Perhaps not, but faith knows that the point of time you prayed initiated the release of the answer even without immediate manifestation. Receiving occurs first in the spiritual realm and then is manifested in the natural. To better illustrate, there's a parable about a fig tree in the book of Mark, which Jesus cursed that no one would ever eat of its fruit again. The results were not seen immediately to the eye like most other miracles Jesus performed however, the tree began to wither from the roots under the ground which was evident the next day. This parable is a reminder that you may not see immediate results in the natural, but in the spiritual realm it's already started and can be considered already done.

Considering a prayer already done requires a different response. Instead of worrying about it or reminding God about it, as if He's forgotten, you need to thank God for the blessing that's on the way. Receiving is admitting it's already done and accepting His response to your prayer. If you're always asking God for the same thing over and over the problem can become that you're no longer receiving (taking into possession) the blessing or miracle. As women, we are built to receive. Therefore, how much more should we have confidence in the truth (believe) that what we've taken into possession (received) will be done. Note: this excludes praying with wrong motives because James 4:3 lets you know that in this case, you do not receive because the things that you desire are to squander on your own pleasures. But when you pray with right motives and believe, you enter into rest knowing that God has heard you and will answer you. In 1 John 5:14 it brings it home telling you this is the confidence that you have in approaching God, that if you ask anything according to His will He hears you. Remove worry and find rest that everything is in God's hands.

Reflection Moment: If you're asking according to God's will, you can have confidence that God will answer you. List what your praying for? Is it according to God's will?

THE BASELINE OF
CONNECTING TO
GOD

Silence

IT RESETS YOUR FOCUS,
RECALIBRATES YOUR
TRIUNE BEING, AND
ALLOWS YOU TO HEAR GOD

- RAIN JOHNSON

- deep dive-

Everything has to do with the condition of the heart. And because
God is concerned about the heart you have to guard your hearts and
minds with prayer, supplication, and with thanksgiving letting your
requests be made known to God (Phil. 4:6-7). The heart is the center
of your physical life and the center of your spiritual life. Therefore, the
motive(s) behind what you do is important because it assigns feeling,
emotion, and intention to what's in the heart prior to your choice or
action. Spiritually, the heart is connected to the mind and all its functions including: what you think about, wonder about, give your attention to, and worry about. Your thoughts need to be right before God.
The heart is also the center of your moral life. The heart condemns you
(1 John 3:19-21) and represents the true nature and character of who

you are. Now, looking closer at emotions, spiritually, we're gifted with an abundance of sensitivity which boosts our spiritual connection and bond with God. Spiritual sensitivity guides you, like a compass, to the call of God (i.e. silence, worship). And emotions enable you physically to bond and connect to your spouse, children, etc.

> The Lord looks at the heart while people look at the outward appearance (1 Sam. 16:7). Be sure that your heart is not full of wickedness. Jeremiah 7:9 says that out of the heart comes evil things, wicked things, and who can know it. Defilement comes from within rather than from without. So, no matter how a person may try to defile you physically, the greater harmful effect comes by allowing it to enter and defile the heart. The heart can be the root of the problem in bad choices. Allow God to do His good work in you. He is greater.

Again, emotions and feelings serve you well within context assisting you to formulate a response to an experience or situation at hand. However, emotions should not rule over your heart *assisting* or mind. You are instructed to put on the spiritual armor which protects you. The battle you're fighting is not physical (flesh) but against principalities (evil spirits) and the rulers of the darkness of this world (Eph. 6:12). An important piece of your armor is the helmet of salvation which protects your mind. Mind translated refers to the heart and soul. The mind contains your decision or judgement. It also holds your knowledge of who God is and who He says you are.

Without protection you are vulnerable to attack(s) on what you know to be true. Understand that you are important to God's plan. Note: the Samaritan woman at the well was searching for true life, which could not be found in the validation of men. Jesus confirmed her worth and value in creation.

When emotions start to rise, take a moment to appraise/evaluate the nature, quality, and importance of your feelings to determine the response. Feelings may be valid for the experience or situation at hand but what you do next determines right versus wrong. Remember, emotions are a strength not an obstacle. It's important in this moment to offer your emotions to God in order to separate you from them to gain clarification. And without responding (action), allow God to reveal the next steps to you. Note: when feelings are agitated by emotions they're usually accompanied by certain physiological changes like increased heartbeat, respiration, and often overt manifestations (i.e. crying or shaking, etc.). Emotions are not meant to manipulate, control behavior, or dominate your ability to make wise decisions. Instead, emotions give you an opportunity to take 'inventory" of feelings. Inventory doesn't equal to an immediate response. Taking inventory provides time to derive to the right reaction to the experience/situation at hand. The response you give can produce life or crush life. Therefore, take the necessary time to receive guidance and produce the response that will give life. Remember, what you know to be true will always outweigh how you feel because spiritual truth overrules emotions. People can call you names all day but when you know the truth of who you are... the response will be different. Exercise self-control by practicing restraint over impulses and emotions. Consistency in this area will lead to self-discipline, along with the ability to make the right decision in the moment. The right choice is measured by God's commandments.

Many times, it's said that women are "too emotional". Emotions connect/bond you with God, mankind and creation. It's your beautiful soul's response to the acknowledgment of The Spirit of God working in you. Emotions are a strength and your way of processing feelings to generate a proper response. You represent the essence of life bringing emotional energy, willpower, and joy. When you walk with God, continue to show evidence that the Spirit of God is at work in your life with love, joy, patience, kindness, goodness, faithfulness, gentleness, and self-control (Gal. 5:22-23) EVEN WHEN trouble comes. Paul, in Romans 5:3-5, wrote of rejoicing even in suffering because of the final fruit that would result in. Your emotions enable you to enjoy all that God has for you. It also allows you to be there for others.

Reflection Moment: How can you apply what you read about emotions to your daily life?

God gives purpose to all creation

God removes thoughts and ideas that attempt to destroy the truth. However, you have to operate with the mind of Christ speaking with authority and living with confidence in God. In other words, walk in the spirit and claim the inheritance of God (Eph. 1:11).

inheritance

The Holy Spirit will teach you ALL things (purpose) and remind you of all that God has said concerning you (John 14:27; Rom. 15:13). To know God's purpose is to know how strong you are and the power you have to withstand forces of lies and deceit. Let your aim be for transformation, redemption, forgiveness, and righteousness. Romans 8:2 says, "Because through Christ Jesus the law of the Spirit of life set me free from the law of sin and death." You are chosen and ordained that you should bring forth fruit and it should remain (John 15:16). Therefore, recognize the good placed inside of you. See your talents and creativity knowing you have all that is needed to be victorious and successful. Focus on what you have and not what you lack. Psalm 34 says, those who seek the Lord will never lack for any good thing. Believe the Word of The Lord!

You are intended to grow and extend beyond self-imposed boarders and into the lives of others; call towards humanity. This is what purpose does… it extends love, support, and encouragement. The Samaritan woman extended herself beyond her boarders and into the lives of those around her. We are told that she left her water jar and ran back to tell everyone who would listen of her encounter. Her encounter not only uncovered her true identity but her worth on the earth which was far more than what she thought. Yes, God knows everything you've done and still chooses to reveal Himself to you. Be the recipient of not only forgiveness but grace, mercy, and love. Be restored back to fulfillment and peace that belongs to you.

> If you allow your emotions or feelings to be led by the body, you subject your total being to the possibility of fulfilling the body's craving(s). God does not dwell where sin resides. Invite God to dwell within and experience true life designed for you.

Reflection Moment: Can you relate to the Samaritan woman at the well? Write down some ways this scripture speaks to you.

-lessons learned-

Purpose will be challenged in this world. In the beginning, God gave one restriction in Genesis 2:16-17 *challenged* "And the Lord God commanded the man, You are free to eat from any tree in the garden but you must not eat from the tree of the knowledge of good and evil, for when you eat from it you will certainly die." Here, the lesson to learn is mankind's tendency to forget their need for fellowship (constant silence; stillness) with God because later in Genesis 3:6 it says, "When the woman saw that the fruit of the tree was good for food and pleasing to the eye, and also desirable for gaining wisdom, she took some and ate it." Perhaps she spoke with God earlier in the day but surly she wasn't communing with God when she was deceived by the serpent (satan) in the garden. Neither was she communing when she gave some to Adam, who also ate from the forbidden tree. The evil orchestrated by satan (opposition to God) deceived the woman. Therefore, you learn that deception turns into disobedience. Disobedience marked the moment woman attempted to live a life apart from God. And disobedience holds consequences. In this particular scenario, Eve's decision catapulted death, both spiritually and physically, into mankind. Let's review the tactics satan used to cause woman to doubt God. Satan caused her to question:

- God's wisdom – compared all the trees showing her that only one tree was forbidden. The goal was to get her to question why God would plant a tree and then tell them they couldn't eat from it. This comparison planted doubt in her mind. Don't doubt God.

• God's word – questioned the truthfulness of God's word. He wanted her to deny God's truthfulness when he told her God was misrepresenting what would really happen if she ate from the tree. The serpent claimed The Creator was not being truthful and the results would give her new knowledge.

• God's character – accused God of wishing to withhold good things from her keeping her ignorant by not eating from the forbidden tree. The enemy of God was charging that God was being selfish not wanting them to have the same knowledge as Him.

You make the choice for yourself

The choice of disobedience was first received through hearing the lie (body), accepting it in her mind (soul), and then receiving the lie as truth (spirit) reversing the original triune order; placing the body first. Recall, receiving is a beautiful part of woman's purpose which was/is under attack. Temptation brings confusion which attempts to disconnect you from God. God is not the author of confusion but of peace (1 Cor. 14:33). Christ's ultimate victory over evil and its manifestation is affirmed (1 Cor. 15:24-28) and nothing can separate us from the love of God in Christ Jesus our Lord (Rom. 8:39). You cannot please God in your own strength. It's only when you allow God to work in you that you receive the desire and power to please God (Phil. 2:13). Within His plan you are covered and move in sync with creation.

Reflection Moment: Obedience is not only hearing God's Word but acting accordingly (Exod. 19:5, Jer. 7:23). What has God been asking you to do that you have not completed?

God desires to give you good things and you must also desire to have the good things God wants to give you. With God you can reclaim your identity, purpose, and success. It's beautiful to know and understand what you really mean to The Creator. Meditate on I Peter 4:10-11 "Each of you should use whatever gift you have received to serve others, as faithful stewards of God's grace in its various forms. If anyone speaks, they should do so as one who speaks the very words of God. If anyone serves, they should do so with the strength God provides, so that in all things God may be praised through Jesus Christ. To him be the glory and the power for ever and ever. Amen."

-triune 3 in 1-

The spirit distinguishes you from inorganic objects/dead organisms. And the spirit reflects, as a mirror, your connection to God who is Spirit. Your reflection should indicate or point out *reflects* God working in your feelings, emotions, attitude, and intentions. Without the Spirit, you do not live a fully purposed driven life. The Spirit renews you imparting power, wisdom, and gives understanding. The Spirit of God is like the wind, you can't see it, but you see its effects and hear the sound. And the Spirit serves as the gateway to the soul. The Holy Spirit will direct your soul to the right decision. The soul receives and processes your feelings generating a response to experiences while marking Holy Spirit (Life) operating within your emotions. Now, just as the body desires and needs nourishment, the soul desires and needs nourishment. The Bible refers to the soul as the hungry, thirsty, satisfied soul (Ps. 107:9, Prov. 27:7, Jer. 31:25). Do not ignore the soul as it points to or marks life (Holy Spirit). Recall, Eve's name meant life because God designed her to embody life and all it offers. Adhere to the gentle tugging of the Spirit so you don't become vulnerable to the opposition of God. Vulnerability turns to despair, incitement, embitterment, unsettlement, suspense, etc. Take time to nourish the soul which hungers and thirsts for the living God, the Word of God, and to have a relationship with God (Ps. 42:2-3). Turn your soul over to God daily.

> Hebrew word ruach and the Greek word pneuma for spirit
> translate "wind" and "breath". These words help us make
> the connection between the spirit, breath and wind.

Often the body is out of order. Especially if the body is leading. This is because you are first spirit clothed with a body. Too often the focus is on the body's form, shape, or desires rather than on God's purpose/design for it. As women we nurture, care for, and support all of mankind not just with our body but with our total being. The body (flesh) has physical needs which can become weak and subject to temptation if not addressed. Weaknesses of the flesh include basic necessities but also include desires of power, sex, and even evil (Prov. 21:10). The Old Testament does not express the idea of body. In the New Testament, basar means flesh, designating the body as a whole. Body can mean earthly existence of an individual which withers away under God's judgment (Isa. 40:6-7) but survives through the covenant of grace (Gen. 9:11-17). The body is the place of proper worship, the temple of the Holy Spirit (I Cor. 6:19-20) which should be disciplined (I Cor. 9:27).

Physical love is a gift from God (Gen. 2:23-24). A man and woman's bond is a deep natural connection, spirit to spirit, and nothing short of a miracle. For women, we spiritually and emotionally cover whom we physically love. Perhaps this is why the effects of a broken relationship cause so much emotional turmoil. God never intended for the bond to be broken and thus we suffer with the consequences of the aftermath. Spiritual conflict occurs   *broken* when we step outside of God's will for life. For example, God instilled the practice of one man with one woman (monogamy);

later emphasized by Jesus (Matt. 19:4-6). Therefore, when sexual sin rules the body it displaces the triune being. Your body belongs to God in which sexual sin cannot abide (1 Cor. 6:12-20). Breaking this bond is compared to a tearing in the soul because it goes against God's intended purpose for marriage. The New Testament provides cases in which divorce is allowed but emotional turmoil or effects are not diminished. Being in agreement with God is the most powerful expression of your entire self. Life gains meaning, fulfillment, and your response(s) to life will be productive.

God satisfies the desires of the soul

-you are-

Purpose requires knowing the truth. The truth is that:
You are formed on God's words and thoughts toward you   *formed*
which supersede all else. You're an individual design with your
own personality, values, and responsibilities but you are also a part of the common thread shared by all women within God's beautiful canvas. This united thread, through Eve, is illuminated as you develop in your relationship with The Creator. Spiritual identity helps support, form, and arrange all other layers of who you are. In Genesis 1:26 God said, "Let us make man in our image, after our likeness; and let them have dominion over the fish of the sea and over the fowl of the air, and over the cattle, and over all the

earth, and over every creeping thing that creepeth upon the earth." Being formed after the likeness of God means you carry the authority and validation to function and prosper on the earth. It means you have immense value and worth.

You are a helper deemed good. In Genesis 2:18 God said, "It is not good that the man should be alone; I will make him an help meet for him." God created you to not only be good but to cause, exist as, and come with good for both mankind and creation. God made woman to be favorable, pleasant, happy, beautiful, delightful, prosperous, understanding, valuable, and morally good. From the beginning, God deemed woman good for man and good to the earth. You bring unity, togetherness, inclusion, incorporation, friendship, aid, and help. Woman never held a negative connotation in God's plan as His final creative act.

> Your first bond is found here... "Before I formed you in the womb I knew you; Before you were born I sanctified you; I ordained you a prophet to the nations" (Jer. 1:5). As you move into living a life of purpose & success, there are a few things you should recall... woman was spiritually connected to God and in position to hear, see, and receive from God. Her soul & heart were right before God. This included her feelings and emotions which were positive and focused on God and His goodness. There was no room for bitterness, hate, or negativity. In other words, when you focus on your relationship with God you fill your space with godly things. But when you remove your focus you open yourselves up to ungodly things. Your heart should reflect God.

Your spirit, soul, and body complement each
other all working together to complete you

You are ordained by God to hold a space/place in creation and mankind. God invested in you and everything God lays His hand(s) on is ordered by His authority and laws. God has extended mercy and grace to us. Instead of God separating Himself completely from us, He has promised to solve the problem of sin and death through the promise of Eve's descendant, Jesus, who would deliver the ultimate crushing blow to satan. Choose to obey and serve God.

You are a receiver. Woman received the breath of God that establishes life and accepted His words and thoughts concerning you. Your first relationship was with God and then you were received by man. You receive by bonding spiritually, emotionally, and then physically. Our womb receives the seed of man and delivers life back to the earth.

You are a carrier of life. Woman carries life physically until it's mature enough to be released into the world. You are created to nurture life in every way. You carry life spiritually molding lives in our relationships. You have the ability to progress life forward with your influence. You are strong in your effectiveness, growth, and energy in creation. You bring life, not take life away. You live and move and have being (Acts 17:28). You represent life which is active, energetic, enthusiastic, etc. and you extend this life to all creation.

You are sensitive. Women are sensitive to the heartbeat of God. Sensitivity makes us aware and in tune to His heartbeat. As a mother to her child, God desires to lavish His love on you (1 John 3:1). Sensitivity enables you to bond with your children. Yes, the "nurture gene" makes you great developers, trainers, protectors, supporters, and encouragers. All women have this gift; child or no child.

In order to live and remain in these truths… you must be recharged by The Spirit of God daily. When you choose to put the mercy, compassion, lovingkindness, steadfast love, and goodness of God before you…you walk by faith in God's truth. In the midst of all doubt or issues of life make the decision to trust God. For He is the Source of all truth.

> *Nurturing is a strength that God provides*
> *(1 Pet. 4:10-11) enabling you to be good caregivers,*
> *disciplinarians, servers, and multitaskers.*

-three-

balance

spiritual balance
| **bal•ance** |

stability produced by even distribution of
triune weight mental and emotional steadiness
a means of judging or deciding

*B*alance balance **balance** is necessary. Women, great multitaskers, usually juggle several tasks at once. However, many times the tasks are not working together to assist us like they should. Instead, we find ourselves burning out because our tasks are no longer preventing failure. Have you taken on some things never intended for you to take on? Balance combines the following: 1) remaining in God's presence (silence) 2) while living (stillness) and 3) mitigating life's unexpected twists and turns with preventive maintenance. Balance requires focus in order to prioritize tasks. Prioritizing is setting, tracking, concentrating, and scheduling your time. Time is limited, so you really need to make the most of it. Balance helps you determine how much time and self you should pour out into each task, along with how to maintain each part of your triune being to remain rejuvenated, refreshed, and ultimately alive. Without balance you pour without being refilled which brings you to a halt. Remember, being alive is more than just breathing; existing. John 6:63 says, "...The Spirit gives life." Life is being active, prepared, functional, and useful.

The body covers our organs that pump life to the body. The spirit covers the seat of our emotions (heart) directing life.

The last thing you want is to find out that more than half the things you're doing in life don't even contribute towards your life's purpose. Life is not meant to be over-burdened, dysfunctional, or causing immobility. You are not guaranteed a pain free life but you are guaranteed a victorious life when you are spiritually connected and balanced. God has placed time, purpose, and destiny all together for His purposes and your good. When was the last time you stopped and took inventory on what you're doing versus what God wants you to do? When you're in sync with the heartbeat of God, He will reveal to you the things that He has for you versus the things you've chosen to take on your own strength. Hearing the heartbeat of God involves removing outside noises which develops a centered life- style, godly habits, attitudes, and moral standards that places God in His proper place in your life. Choose to be aligned with God.

Spiritual maintenance comes through The Word of God, meditation, prayer, and worship. Physical maintenance, also important, comes through healthy eating, exercise, and hydration. Without balance in these places you can easily be exposed to a life in "neutral" which no one should remain in. Neutral is a drifting place where you're easily moved by situations or surroundings, lacking power to determine your own momentum or growth. It's also a place where you are vulnerable to the body (flesh) dominating. Losing focus on God lowers your value and position. Paul, in Galatians, provides instructions saying, "...live by the Spirit, and you will not gratify the desires of the sinful nature." Your instructions are to be filled with the Spirit (Eph. 5:18) and to be spiritually minded (Rom. 8:6). Again, being spiritually filled is the first step to being balanced. There's no way around it. Paul reminds us in 2 Corinthians 4:18: "...we do not look at the things which are seen, but at the things which are not seen. For the things which are seen are temporary, but the things which are not seen are eternal."

Reflection Moment: What choices and decisions have you made to be aligned with the heartbeat of God?

Be balanced and steady in an otherwise unstable world

-stable & sensitive-

Women are designed to be stable. Stability is a result of balance. However, you support mankind and creation in a world that has become unstable. So while you embody security, strength, support, and firmness...in an unstable world these are the very things that you too yearn for yourself. This is why it's very important to remain in si-lence (God's presence) while living (stillness) so that you're receiving back from God what was poured out; remaining stabled and balanced. Balance involves total self; not part of self. It's complete trust in God to guide you with His insight. Yes, He will instruct you. Just like your body registers when we're full, your spirit also knows when we're full. You only experience your best life when you're positioned correctly with God. Philippians 4:7 says, "And the peace of God, which transcends all understanding, will guard your hearts and your minds in Christ Jesus." God will give you peace.

God was in the beginning of the world (Gen. 1:1) and God will be there in the end. He is "Alpha and Omega, the first and the last, the beginning and the end" (Rev. 22:13 NRSV). And when you remember God's place in life and in the universe... everything else falls into its proper place.

Stabilization is necessary in this unstable world

Your acute mental and emotional sensibility helps you to respond to the feelings of others. This is why so much of what you see, hear, and feel affects you. Sensitivity is a strength, not a weakness. In fact, I'll go as far to say it's a super-power to perceiving the movement of The Holy Spirit. Your capacity for compassion is extensive. And is only a problem when you get "hung-up" or stuck in feelings because it can cause wild fluctuations in your emotions which is an indication that the body is leading. And guess what? The enemy of God knows that if you get "hung-up" or stuck in feelings you are easily pained, annoyed, etc. ultimately making you unstable and not producing life. Resist all attempts of satan to play on your feelings. Embrace God's truth. Put focus back on God. And let nothing move you from the will of God but instead give yourself fully to the work of the Lord (1 Cor. 15:58). Remember, God's thoughts toward you are of peace, not evil, and for a good future (Jer. 29:11).

-authority-

Exercise the gift of authority God has given you. If you don't understand your authority on the earth, you *excercise* will struggle with your authority in the spirit and balance. Authority is being able to determine, command, and settle issues or experiences that arise in life. This is not acquired in your own human effort but rather given to you by God. Know there is no obstacle that you cannot overcome with God. You have the power to conquer with perseverance, in the cause of Christ. Authority was initially given to man and woman to have dominion over creation and every "creepeth" thing on earth (fish of the sea, fowl of the air, cattle, and every beast of the earth where there if life). Every "creepeth" thing includes the enemy of God (satan). That's good information right there! Authority is important because it brings victory. In 2 Corinthians 10:3-5, you are told that even though you walk in the flesh you do not war after the flesh, and that the weapons of your warfare are mighty through God to pull down strong holds. For those governed by flesh are hostile to God and cannot please Him (Rom. 8:7-8, 1 Cor. 2:14). Remember that the flesh is weak and vulnerable to sin. Remain physically in the flesh but do not live according to the flesh (Gal. 2:20). You must constantly check the flesh with self-discipline (balance) as you are led by The Spirit.

> God demonstrates His power and the Bible provides examples of His power through delivering Israel from Egyptian slavery (Exod. 4:21, Exod. 9:16, Exod. 15:6, Exod. 32:11) in the conquest of Canaan (Ps. 111:6) in the power to judge and the power to forgive sin just to name a few.

The center and pivot point of life must be greater than self

Victory comes by releasing the worlds distorted view of you. In the book of Exodus women gave their mirrors, which once belonged to their captors, to be melted down and used to make the bronze laver or bronze basin. This laver was one of the furnishings required by God in the outer courts of the tabernacle, between the temple and alter, which held water for washing or cleansing (Exod. 30:18, 38:8). These mirrors came from a place of bondage and represented feelings of defeat, low value, and mistreatment. The melting down is symbolic of God removing the old image or the way they saw themselves and providing a place of cleansing as a renewed image of how God truly sees woman. Wash away the worlds distorted view of you. In order to reach destiny, it requires that you see yourself in a new way. The same way God does. Remember that the body is a temple of the Holy Spirit in which you are to honor God with (1 Cor. 6:19-20). It doesn't matter what other people said about you or what they did to you. God calls you righteous (Rom. 5:1-11). And it's God's mirror that matters. He will help you make decisions and choices that reflect your true beauty and heart. This is reclaiming authority.

As a believer understand that there will be trials and afflictions, but the Lord will deliver you out of them all (Ps. 34:19). Isaiah 59:19 tells you that when the enemy comes in like a flood, the Spirit of the Lord will lift up a standard against him and he must leave. See, you're not weak or defeated. As a believer you must understand the authority you have in Christ and there is no other option outside of victorious. In Matthew 28:18-19, Jesus said, "All power is given unto me in heaven and in earth. Go ye therefore, and teach all nations, baptizing them in the name of the Father, and of the Son, and of the Holy Ghost." You have The Lord backing you up as you proclaim His love to a world that needs to know it. And if that's not enough, Luke 10:19 says, "Behold, I give unto you power to tread on serpents and scorpions, and over all the power of the enemy: and nothing shall by any means hurt you." It's your job to submit yourself to God and resist the devil because he will have to depart from us (James 4:7). Jesus came to assure you that you have the power to win.

God's living water offers true life now on earth and eternal life with Him in Heaven. He desires to show you His beauty. However, being human and sinful, there's this bad habit of wanting to grasp tangible things (people, money, etc.) instead of grasping for spiritual things. You are so conditioned to seeing with your eyes, which serve their purpose, instead of opening your spiritual eyes. Romans 12:2 says, "Do not conform to the pattern of this world, but be transformed by the renewing of your mind. Then you will be able to test and approve what God's will is – his good, pleasing and perfect will." Let us now honor God by remaining in the realm of the Spirit (Rom. 8:9) and living (Rom. 8:11-17). Life is at its fullest when lived according to God's intentions and not used to search for material and cultural goods (Mark 8:34-37). Sin causes weakness, and inferiority from who you truly are. Jesus, who came to fulfill the law, restores you to your rightful place in creation and the earth. Receive the Living Water.

You can overcome everything and anything

Reflection Moment: 2 Corinthians 10:3-5 tells you that even though you walk in the flesh you do not war after the flesh. What does this scripture mean to you?

You have the authority and power to accept or deny experiences. It really comes down to the way you process these events that makes the difference. While it's true that God allows both good and *process* bad experiences to happen, that doesn't mean they are His perfect will. You can either gain knowledge and wisdom from what you've encountered, or you can be resentful and angry. How much an experience affects you is totally up to you. Your decision will either affect your ability to grow and live, or it can propel your willpower and trust in God knowing He is with you and in control of all things. Mitigation limits/lessens the force or intensity a situation has on you, especially unpleasant situations. In the Bible, Esther was a queen whose faith was tested. She went from being an orphan to a queen. But there was a major moment where mitigation through fasting, prayer, and accepting the situation presented before her was necessary. Reclaiming her authority and power as God's woman, she took the necessary leap of faith which ultimately saved her people as she found favor with the King.

Being led by The Spirit of God is crucial; as you are spirit

Experiences inflicted upon you by the enemy are ultimately to stop you. John 10:10 tells us that "The thief comes only to steal and kill and destroy. I came that they may have life and have it abundantly." Nothing the enemy promises or takes you through is out of concern for you. No, the goal is to stifle your gifts, talents, and hinder your journey. This could be why you've gone through so much in your life. The enemy hopes that if he can get you to concentrate on the pain of it all you won't be able to think, reason, or focus on anything else but the pain. Don't let negative experiences or mental attacks crush your soul or spirit. Don't build up walls that keep you in self-inflicted bondage. Remember, God's plan for creation includes and involves you. He wants to bless you with His resources so that you can be successful for His Glory. You have purpose not only with mankind but in your relationship with God. Embrace your true stature without underestimating any part of who you are. You have God's signature on your canvas. Have confidence in God which will enable you to be bold, more creative, increase self-esteem, and have an overall well-being.

> Encountering God brings feelings of warmth, complete peace, and emotional relief (to name a few). Similar to worship, your response may vary in the presence of God but the feeling or sense felt by all is an awareness and oneness with The Creator.

Reflection Moment: Harm to the body doesn't have to permeate into the spirit. How can you exercise authority over events that happen in life?

-*imbalance*-

Woman was not created to lack balance. Just the opposite, she was created perfectly balanced and connected to God. She embraced true beauty, inward and outward, with only God as her judge. And in His presence (in silence) she is empowered...you are empowered. Be clear there is no doubt that woman held her place down in the world. And all was well until... deception entered. Deception which distracts balance causing us to question God and our true place in *deception* creation. This will always lead you away from the presence of God and His perfect will. There is no room to remove your focus off of God. Yet there's still a tendency to try to balance life in your own strength. Recall, your own strength is body led; not spirit led. And you know how that's going to end. The results do not progress you forward successfully. Sure, there may be movement, but it's compromised movement. Whenever you attempt to spin opposite of purpose there will be conflict. Conflict which causes you to second guess almost every decision and area of life. Just remember it's never too late to find balance.

Too much weight on any one side of your triune being causes imbalance, hindering full potential. Imbalance affects your mind, emotions, judgment, and decision making. Imbalance carries stress rather than the peace, confidence, calm, and happiness you're meant to have. As women, we tend to overload ourselves with responsibilities. We pour ourselves into others, neglecting or forgetting to love self and take time for self-care. Note: you have to "take time" because so many other things/people are aggressively competing for it. This is why you often find yourself burned out, frustrated, and disappointed. You simply cannot do it all! You must use your ability to judge with truth and wisdom; discernment. In other words, differentiate between truth and error, right and wrong, and what should and should not be taken on. Instead take time to pray and meditate before committing yourself. And then once committed, conduct daily checks on your commitments with God to mitigate misalignment because commitments can be for a season for a reason. There's a gift of saying "no" which is required along the way, especially to things that do not align with your purpose. Again, you don't want to take on what is not meant for you. Another sign of imbalance is when you no longer feel comfortable with who God created you to be. You have to know that God created you perfect. Don't take your focus off of what God says about you. Steer clear of negative people with negative viewpoints.

Balance provides strength, security, and safety

Reflection Moment: What distractions cause you to question yourself? Are you being led away from God's presence and perfect will?

Finally, invest time and attention into each area of your spirit, soul, and body. This will keep you present and spirit forward. Invest in your future, not your past, which needs your full attention. Remain focused and maintain your course always seeking truth.

-motives-

Knowing the reason why you do what you do should be looked at closer. This brings clarification to the motive(s) behind your actions. Because many times, you do things for appearance's sake, but in reality your heart isn't in what you're doing. It's just going through the motions. Even a good deed may not really be a good deed if it's not performed with a right heart and intentions. Are you doing things with a right heart? God weighs the motives behind the actions and great emphasis is on the attitude by which your actions stem. Matthew 6:1 says, "Take heed to yourself, that you do not your righteousness before men, to be seen of men." And Jesus said, "I say unto you, you have your reward." What you do should not be to receive applause or recognition from people but rather from God. 2 Corinthians 5:10 tells you that God receives the things you've done in your body whether they be good or evil. And it's God who sees what you do in secret and who will reward you openly (Matt. 6:4).

Be aware of snares and entanglements. They keep you anxious and seeking approval from others. It's really a form of bondage. The Hebrew word "mokesh" refers to bait or lure used to capture prey. This is when you find yourself being moved by the opinions of others as your reasoning for doing something. Your reasoning for why you do something should not be out of the fear of others not liking you, loving you, or accepting you. Prov. 29:25 declares, "Fear of man will prove to be a snare, but whoever trusts in the LORD is kept safe." And then rest in God's approval knowing you are His. In 2 Timothy 1:7 you are told that God has not given you a spirit of fear but of power, love, and self-control. Therefore, let all the things be done to glorify God seeking only His approval which leads to life.

> Truth is reflected in God's commandments and in life. Psalm 139:13-14 speaks of God 's possession over you even when you were in our mother's womb He covered and held you. Truth is in God's nature of being faithful through his acts in creation, election, and redemption. Truth is in His faithfulness to forgive you of your sins and cleanse you from all unrighteousness (1 John 1:9) and faithful not to tempt you above what you're able (1 Cor. 10:13). God is reliable, steadfast, dedicated, dependable, and worthy of trust. Choose not to entertain negativity or words contrary to the truth. Distractions seek to consume your time and attention which weaken and deceive.

Think about it, God knows the depth of the sea and interior of the earth...surely, He knows the depth and intentions of your heart and motives. You yourself cannot understand purpose or life apart from God. He provides spiritual and emotional meaning into the uncharted and charted areas of your heart, mind, and soul. When you increase spirituality, the Spirit allows you to see life from another point of view. This gives you the desire to live for God and not for people or things. It's only when you minimize spirituality that you maximize imbalance, heavily relying on your own limited human ability. Constantly filter out distractions and deception. Reduce the noise allowing purpose to be louder. Be engaged in life and let the reason behind why you do something be God-centered. Only then are you genuinely able to encourage, elevate, and pray for all mankind.

Reflection Moment: The spirit chases those things that please God. Take a moment to reflect on what you're chasing. Is the spirit leading you?

-maintenance-

Self-preventative maintenance is the care and service you give yourself to maintain and operate a successful life. Regularly performing internal and external checks lessens the likelihood of failing. Self-care is especially important before taking care of others. By looking for early signs of instability, anxiety, or fluctuations in your feelings or emotions, you can avoid an unexpected break down and provide the opportunity for correction. It's not a question of *if* a break down will happen...it's a matter of *when* a break down will happen. This is because we're human with flaws and constantly learning how to maintain and live life. Before moving forward, let's review a few things on spirit versus body. You know by now the spirit should lead because the spirit knows God, connects with God, and understands the path to destiny and purpose. And that the body (natural flesh) has an intrinsic habit of being selfish, self-centered, and covetousness, along with other "fleshy" desires (i.e. greed). The body tends to follow after things that please it. The spirit is living water; life and fulfillment. The body is temporary satisfaction; ending in crisis. Romans 8:6-8 tells you that being carnally minded is death but being spiritually minded is life and peace and that those who are in the flesh cannot please God. Therefore, wherever your focus is will become your desire (soul). While you need to pay attention to your body, within balance, your primary attention should be centered on God.

The spirit and body should be healthy and balanced. Just as we need to eat, get proper sleep, and exercise... *healthy* the spirit also needs to worship, submit, and connect to God our Father. In James 2:15-16 it says, "Suppose a brother or sister is without clothes and daily food. If one of you says to him, "Go, I wish you well; keep warm and well fed,' but does nothing about his physical needs, what good is it?" If you totally ignore the body's needs, you only suppress the spirit resulting in standing condemned before God. Jesus often addressed and healed the flesh of the inflicted before ministering to the spirit of a person. All areas of your being (spirit, soul, and body) need prioritization and nutrition; working together. This is balance.

Reflection Moment: Early signs that self-preventative maintenance is required are: anxiety, insecurity, uncertainty, volatility, hesitation, frailty, and restlessness.

Nourishing the spirit is important because it regulates and strengthens your connection and relationship with God. *nourishing* A healthy life produces a healthy lifestyle in which habits, attitudes, desires, and morals all work together to represent your beautiful role as God's woman. Keep a spiritual ear open to God so that you can stand (silence) and walk (stillness) in righteousness; balanced. Proverbs 31, speaks of a woman clothed with strength and dignity, and how she laughed at the days to come and spoke with wisdom. Faithful instruction was on her tongue, and she watched over the affairs of her household not eating the bread of idleness. Balance is also utilizing talents that fulfill you, give peace, and extend you to others.

Practice the art of gratitude. This begins by acknowledging everything God has done for you even though you don't deserve it all. Gratitude pleases God and somehow changes you in the process. You can show gratitude by doing good to both self (self-care) and all mankind. Rejoice always, pray without ceasing, and in everything give thanks (1 Thess. 5:16-18). But let's be real, it's hard to give thanks for the problems, however, you can give thanks even in the midst of them. Sure, you can. You can thank Him if only for what's left! Just knowing God loves you and is in control no matter what you encounter. Remember, God is working all things for your good even when you can't see it… God is guiding your steps. Don't take anything for granted. Gratitude should be your response to God's provisions, deliverance, grace, faithfulness, and concrete acts. Gratitude is a powerful means of drawing closer to God. Keep a positive mindset by surrounding yourself with positive like-minded people.

Balance prevents total neglect

A successful life does not necessarily appear in tangible forms (money, houses, jewelry, etc.) because God doesn't master in temporary satisfaction. God masters in victory that "sticks." His outcomes stay for the duration without fading, rusting, or tarnishing. The difference between the world's victory vs. God's victory is that God's win is perfect, complete, and lacks nothing. In fact, it often gives more than expected. This is spiritual wholeness. In Matthew 4:58 you are told to be perfect, as God is perfect. Your relationship with God makes it possible to be victorious/perfect. And the proper response should be whole-hearted obedience which renews you.

God is: Good (Rev. 15:4) God hates evil (Ps. 5: 4-5) God loves you (1 John 4:7-11) God has made it possible for you to know Him personally through His son Jesus Christ (John 3: 16-17). And while many reject the existence of God, yet and still they substitute the true and living God with false gods (spirits of their ancestors, trees, rivers, mountains, false gods and goddesses, etc.) in His place. Why? Because you are made to worship. God is full of goodness, love, mercy, and grace. I understand this may be a different version of God from what you've heard of but if this is an accurate picture it means that God cares about you personally, which is an idea that is just too compelling to walk away from.

God is in the intricate finely woven details of your life. He knows the exact number of hairs on your head, grains of sand on the beach, and stars in the galaxy. God knows the path to a successful life, both now and later in the afterlife. You must constantly press into understanding God's view of the universe and creation. Isaiah 40:12-13 speaks of God measuring the waters in the palm of His hand and meting out the heavens with the span. It speaks to how He weighed the mountains and measured the dust of the earth to form man, then taking the right portion of man to then form woman. Yes, in every detail of everything...God is there, woven into the foundation of the earth, holding up the heavens and the universe. God balances it all. Surely, He can show you how to balance your life. Therefore, continue to walk and operate within God's commandments, engaged in life, and reclaiming your rightful place. Seek to understand and manage stress better which makes you more productive. When you're productive, you produce an effect in creation and affect upon all mankind. Use your authority and power to reduce and defeat the greatest adversary, satan, who comes to steal, kill, and destroy. In addition, the adversary relentlessly accuses God's children continually. Victory is remaining balanced even in the shuffle of everyday living, remaining centered, and staying focused.

-lessons learned-

There are lessons to be learned from the past. Eve, taught us not to be manipulated into bypassing the commandments of God. She was convinced, by satan, that God didn't really provide the particulars or specifics to His commands, when in fact He did. Eve's sin stemmed from her desire for the fruit (lust of the flesh), seeing the tree (lust of the eyes), and thinking she could be smarter than God (pride of life). These desires didn't come from God. The pride of life is defined as anything leading to arrogance, ostentation, pride of self, presumption, or boasting. In 1 John 2:15 it's clear that if anyone loves the world, they cannot love The Father. That kind of says it all! You're to resist the temptation of disobeying God. This is accomplished by recognizing tools satan uses to lure you away from God. These tools are: lusting after the flesh (sexual gratification, gluttony, drugs, etc.), lusting after "things" you surround yourself with ("things" which harden hearts to the desire for God) and temptations of the pride of life which is the very sin that ejected satan out of heaven. There are lessons to be learned from satan who desired to be God and no longer a servant of God (Isa. 14:12-15).The pride of life spurs satan to lure you away from God with the ultimate goal of getting you to elevate self (the body or flesh) and fulfill personal earthly desires.

In order to remain aligned, you must remain connected and balanced which guides you to victory and life. Too many women are not truly communing with God, finding themselves functioning on fumes and existing not truly living the life God intended. Consider if you will, the spinning top as it spins around the rotation axis giving it angular momentum. A perfectly balanced and upright spinning top achieves this angular momentum after a source causes it to start spinning and it will keep spinning until an external source acts upon it (i.e. gravity). Likewise, spiritual balance keeps you upright, active, and living. It's up to you not to allow external sources/forces to stop your progress. Stay in communion with God; via silence and stillness. Yes, I get it life happens! But the life God offers naturally keeps you moving forward leveling distractions. A distraction's purpose is to remove balance gradually until you ultimately are no longer active. However, if you remain connected (balanced) even on bad days, the Holy Spirit will intervene overpower outside forces and give you strength to overcome.

God laid out basic fundamentals concerning us

In art there is a technique on the surface where lines converge in order to give the illusion of depth and distance. In life, an illusion is not reality. Often, you want to appear as if you have it all together. No one is that deep that they don't struggle with some of life's obstacles! And we all struggle to determine the priorities in our life. Balance is understanding that you need to present and yield your spirit, soul, and body daily to God as they function and interact together. This is a time for assessment. The long-term goal is to achieve uninterrupted balance and spiritual growth.

Reflection Moment: Finding the heartbeat of God is being present with creation, the universe, and self. It's inviting God to fill you spiritually taking control of your heart, mind, and emotions. Take a moment to be present and then write a little bit about the experience.

Your struggle is not contending with your roles and responsibilities… it's the struggle against spiritual powers and world forces of wickedness in the supernatural places (Eph. 6:12). If satan can throw you off balance you'll be stressed, over extended, have lack of focus, and frustrated. Remember in both challenging and good moments, pause and recall all of God's great spiritual truths. And in case you don't know what spiritual truths I'm referring to, they are: whatever is true, whatever is honorable and worthy of respect, whatever is right and confirmed by God's word, whatever is pure and wholesome, whatever is lovely and brings peace, whatever is admirable and of good repute; if there is any excellence, if there is anything worthy of praise, think continually on these things, center your mind on them, and implant them in your heart (Phil. 4:8). The risk of falling into frustration, confusion, or misdirection by surrendering to temporary solutions or quick fixes is just too high. Stay on the right path and make the right choice(s). As a great multi-tasker you have the ability to quiet all chambers of your mind, offer them up, and enter into a reunion with God while doing everything you need to do; stillness. Invest in your spirit to refuel and refocus for the greater good of the whole body and everybody you come in contact with.

You're trying to fit "life" into the 24hour day. But when a sense of work-life balance is lost, that's the time to pause and reflect on how much time you've spent actually living versus recharging throughout the day. Take inventory of the areas you may have neglected. For example: Did you pray, meditate, spend time with God, worship, etc.? Did you eat, exercise, sleep, etc.?

In the world of art, I found it interesting that balancing is a composition or placement of designs, as figures, forms, or colors to produce an artistic integrated whole portrait. Similarly, in the spirit, balancing is reclaiming God's placement of purpose as His woman and daughter. And then the mother, sister, wife, friend, etc. that He's blessed you to be all producing and agreeing with God's plan for your life. Purpose is strong, weighted, and bold. Purpose is not weak, frail, or bashful. Finally, believe spiritual truths in order to keep balance/placement in God's plan. For we, who believe, walk in His truth and light.

-*authenticity*-

God placed His signature on your triune portrait, foundation, making you His original WOA, and your actions *actions* should reflect your authenticity. For a true authentic woman is properly aligned with God's image of her. She understands her worth, knows how to operate within purpose, and realizes she cannot be truly successful nor victorious apart from God. Being authentic involves understanding your nature and the things you can CHANGE and CANNOT CHANGE. What you cannot change is: God's laws, the past, history, weather, someone who doesn't want to change, who you are related to, or human needs. You cannot change the past, but you can learn from it choosing to change the present and future. Change happens when you believe you are enough to accomplish the plans of God you feel you are called to. Change involves work and prioritization. Now, what you can change is: who you worship, the path you take, role models, behavior, responses, choices, habits, impulses, responsibility, who to trust or blame, when and how you use your power, how you spend your time, how you apply strengths and talents, how you apply your initiative, commitment, focus, promises, level of nutrition and fitness, integrity, forgiveness, doing better or not to do better. You control how you treat others, react to others, formulate opinions of others, and your relationship with others, etc. to name a few. But here again, without God leading your life, the flesh greatly influences the things you can change.

*Remember, life began in the spirit and separation from the spirit is separation from the authentic you.

You express The Creator's love on canvas.

Foundation is important. Just as an artist can purchase the best paints in the world they aren't any good if they're applied *art* to something that won't last. The canvas, foundation, must be of the highest quality. It must be stretched tightly enough or pulled skew so that the grain doesn't get distorted. If the canvas weave is not right, it can overwhelm the fine details. And so, just as a prepared art canvas is crucial...so too is our spiritual core and connection. The spirit must be maintained in order to receive the next layer God has prepared for you. A strong spiritual connection provides wisdom, understanding, counsel, power, and knowledge needed for life. And fine details lead up to authenticity without fear, anxiety, or shame. Finally, authenticity reveals your:

- Image - how you see yourself
- Stature - level of achievement
- Value - relative worth, merit, or importance
- Belief - confidence in the truth
- Goals - results and achievements directed toward your successful end
- Behavior - your response patterns in given circumstances

The Word tells you that you're "made in His image" (Gen. 1:26) being "fearfully and wonderfully made" (Ps. 139:14). His thoughts toward you are countless as the sand on the seashore (Ps. 139:17-18). You are His treasured possession (Exod. 19:5). And He wants to offer you more than your earthy father ever could (Matt. 7:11). Because He is the perfect Father (Matt. 5:48). God's plan for your future has always been filled with hope (Jer. 29:11). God demonstrated that He is for you, not against you (Rom. 8:31). And wants to show you great and marvelous things (Jer. 33:3). He is able to do more for you than you could possibly imagine (Eph. 3:20).

Reflection Moment: God is always in control. Nothing escapes His watch. You must keep and exercise your faith. For nothing is accomplished without faith. Write a few faith goals below starting with "I will".

God reveals the truth about Himself in His word

-love-

Love today is often short lived. People are too quick to say, "I never loved you, or I fell out of love with you." Do you know what love is or how to love? Divine love is more than a feeling, it's a decision, a commitment, an act of the will superseding personal preferences. This kind of love does not grow cold or diminish like human feelings so often do. Human feelings are important but they often, by themselves, are driven by personal preferences making them deficient to express divine love. You are instructed to love the Lord your God which is *extend* your binding duty, commitment, promise, and obligation. This includes a desire to do good towards others (charitableness, compassion, kindness). Divine love is giving of yourself. In this love, godly love, you not only give but also receive as His presence is with you. You can see the ultimate sacrifice of love which was exemplified through the offering of the heavenly Father who gave His son on your behalf. This offering made salvation available to all who believe (John 3:16). Yes, God Himself provided a lamb, a sacrifice for your sin. Amen. God's love is faithful, and He does not give up on you. Now this may be hard to wrap your head around if you look at the concept of the world's love, but reflect on who God is (1 John 3:2). God is a spirit (John 4:24). And through the spirit you can fully experience His love towards you.

For God is Love and whoever does not love does not know God (I John 4:8). So, with that being said, when you truly know and love God you will extend and show this love to mankind and creation. God's love is faithful, constant, affectionate, and dependable.

Love bonds you with God, who nourishes and refills you, so you can pour back into mankind. Yes, love is an inseparable aspect of your whole design. This could be why you expect love from mankind to be reciprocated in order to keep/maintain the bond. And this also could be why love released causes so much grief. God never intended for bonds to be broken however, because of sin (disobedience to God) you endure grief as the consequence. Real love is loyal and benevolent concern for the well-being of another. God's love is reliable, faithful, and present to the very end. In the teaching of Paul in the book of Corinthians, he associated love with faith and hope, declaring that love is the greatest. Love builds up. Love is patient and kind, not jealous or boastful, not arrogant or rude. *It does not dishonor others. Love is not selfish, irritable, or resentful. Love does not rejoice at wrong but in the right. Love bears, believes, hopes, and endures all things (I Cor. 13:4-7). Love is a part of balance which works to keep us from falling over.

> \We need to take more time to love God and self. A bond takes time to create, and it takes time to release. Regarding relationships, loving in the flesh only gets us in trouble especially in relationships. Get to know a person spiritually and emotionally first as it provides a true and deep sense of who the person is before initiating a physical bond. Love is supposed to provide safety which we desire and which God provides.

We all like to receive good things but remember sometimes good can come through loving discipline. God's discipline is not to embarrass you but to save your soul from the grips of death and hell. You have to trust God, especially in moments when you don't understand His ways. Trusting God provides rest for the soul during difficult times. Choose to believe everything is in God's hands. Don't be shaken by what it looks like in the moment. Cast down the lies from the enemy with the truth of God's Word. When you operate in the spirit, you bring forth "new life" or "renewed life" to yourself and to others. Yes, the spiritual realm and physical realm co-exist, but they are not equal. Being out of balance occurs when you suppress your spiritual growth to elevate physical wants. It takes wisdom, good judgement, and both mental/emotional stability to remain balanced.

You are not privy to purpose in its fullness all at once

Meditation Point –

Here's a little exercise: Take a deep breath. Look to the heavens. Sense the ground beneath you. Inhale – sense the air surrounding you understanding that you are not merely inhaling oxygen but taking in the very breath of God. Exhale - hearing the breath of God being released from your being in the atmosphere. Realize, you hold life given to you as a gift. It is God and God alone who defines you. And beside your name it is God who puts the words to define you. Words that explain who you are, your purpose, value, and destiny. God's Spirit fills your body and reigns over you. Yes. Allow your spirit to yield to the Spirit of God. And then wait for the answer.

-four-

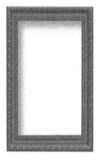

the mind

Mind

| **mind** |

the part, substance, or process that reasons,
thinks, feels, wills, perceives, judges, etc.
conscious and unconscious mental processes
intellect or understanding from faculties of
feeling and willing

We are living in stressful perilous times. In a world drunken with delusions, human depravity, and lawlessness. And right now, the important thing is that you don't lose your mind. In Romans 12:2 you are instructed to not be conformed to this world but be transformed by the renewal of your mind (soul) and that by testing you will be able to discern what is the will of God; good, acceptable, and perfect. Testing comes by way of experiences. Now, in order to discern the will of God, you must first guard your thinking by immersing yourself in truth which will keep you stedfast and unmoveable in the work of the Lord. A sound mind is a delivered and healed mind from chaos and despair (2 Tim. 1:7). The Greek word for "sound mind" stems from a verb meaning "to be made safe". Isn't that what every woman wants to feel? Safety is found being under the submission of the Spirit of God which requires moral discipline. Discipline to change your mind and discipline to change what you fill your mind with.   *safety*

Choose to go to the true source of wisdom - God

Choices originate from your decision-making ability. They tell of your self-control, thoughts, and emotions. Without choices, life would have no meaning...you'd be a programmed robot. A choice always has another option or alternative. And the action that follows a choice, being response, not only represents the choice you've selected but also your understanding of who you are. Let that sink in. A response encompasses core beliefs to include lifestyle, religious beliefs, morals, etc. If your mind is severely limited, restricted, or blocked by internal or external circumstances you may not deliver the proper response. And an improper response runs the risk of going against the commandment of God and being disconnected spiritually. You don't want this. In Ephesians 5:15-16 you are told to be careful of how you live and to not be like the unwise but to be as the wise making the most of every opportunity as you are living in evil times. This is not the time to produce regrettable and disappointing outcomes. Another hindrance can be having too many options, which leads to confusion and indifference. God is not the author of confusion (1 Cor 14:33). Therefore, let your mind be submitted unto God. Check the following before making decisions:

1. **Balance.** Especially when emotions are high; both positive or negative. This is key while processing emotions and shifting through choices. This can be difficult but not impossible if strong physiological changes like increased heartbeat, respiration, crying, or shaking begin. Balance restores calm and is retrieved via prayer, meditation, and worship which re-centers the mind providing necessary guidance in difficult moments. If you are not balanced, don't make decisions until you are.

2. **The Word of God.** This is a must. This will guide you to make a better-informed decision. For example, the Word instructs you not to go against the commandments of God.

3. **Risk vs. gain.** Assess if the risks are greater and the outcomes are only minor positives. This helps determine whether the

option being contemplated should be avoided in favor of a better one. Be sure to think ahead and be prepared to accept responsibility for whatever the outcome is.

Ten Commandments:

You shall have no other Gods before me

You shall not make for yourselves an idol

You shall not misuse the name of the LORD your God

Remember the Sabbath day by keeping it holy

Honor your father and your mother

You shall not murder

You shall not commit adultery

You shall not steal

You shall not give false testimony

You shall not covet

-discontent-

Discontentment and disobedience are a choice you make. Exercising the choice to disobey God makes pain and suffering a reality. However, the other reality is found in God's love when you choose to ask forgiveness. For every choice there is an alternative or another option. This being the point of a choice. God desires that you repent and turn from wicked ways (2 Chron. 7:14). Preventing disobedience requires you to guard your mind discerning good from evil and fear the Lord, which is to hate pride, arrogance, evil behavior, and perverse speech (Prov. 8:13). Removing evil from the equation allows you to discern God's desire in the moment. You are instructed to distinguish between holy and the unholy; between unclean and the clean (Lev. 10:10). It's key to understand and overcome weaknesses of the mind and emotions because we all have a measure of weakness; even the strongest of us. The last thing you want is to become imprisoned to deception. Therefore, turn to the instructions in the book of Ephesians and put on the full armor of God so that you can stand *full armor* your ground against the devil who seeks to destroy you.

This armor is the defense (action) you take in your spiritual life which is the: belt of truth, breastplate of righteousness, shoes of peace, shield of faith, helmet of salvation, sword of the spirit being the word of God, and praying at all times in the spirit.

A restless desire or craving for something that you don't have is discontent. This greedy internal dissatisfaction demands that you change an external circumstance to satisfy the need. This never works out because it's always wanting more of everything, and nothing is ever enough. Discontent is draining. It's usually followed with depression and envy if not dealt with. Other weakness is lacking judgement and good sense. However, take heart because the spirit is here to help you in your weakness. In Philippians 4:11 Paul says, "I have learned in whatever situation I am to be content." Your contentment should not be based on circumstances but rather God's promises. Godliness with contentment is great gain (1 Tim. 6:6). Refusal to be content can take you to great extremes of searching for the meaning of life and self. This restless craving will wear down the mind and open the door for deception to creep in. Eve, in Genesis 3 fell prey to enticement and a lie. Just remember that it's at these times you were so weakened by sin, Christ died for you (Rom. 5:6). He knew you were unable to save yourself.

A God centered-mind empowers you to own your mind, eliminate confusion, establish a position, and control your thoughts/decisions/judgements which all confirm your value. This kind of mind responds positively generating right responses and remains unshaken on the journey of life.

Meditation Point:

The body and mind connection are strong. An estimated 50-70% of visits to the doctor for physical illness are attributed to psychological factors according to the APA Center for Psychology and Health. Right choices and right decisions are best made when operating under the right power and authority - God. In Romans, you are told that there is no authority except from God and you possess authority only as the Lord gives it.

As free-willed beings you have power of
choice to make your own decisions

Reflection Moment: Are you struggling with weakness in the mind? What steps are you going to make to be healed from that?

-*mind* & *heart*-

The mind is the center of intellectual activity, which manifests in thought, perception, memory, emotion, will, and imagination; includes conscious and unconscious cognitive processes. Keeping the mind centered, or focused, from the inception of a thought is important. Philippians 4:7 says, "And the peace of God [the result of this will be the peace o God], which passeth all [human] understanding, shall keep your hearts and minds through Christ Jesus." When you think about it, it's amazing that one single negative thought can take root and grow in the mind. And it carries weight pulling you down until you find yourself burdened and struggling to control your thoughts. However, if you make it your priority to understand the power you truly have to control your thoughts, even in a world full of constant distractions and negative forces, you can be victorious in your thoughts and mind. Negative opposing forces do not have to render you incapable of functioning as designed at full capacity.

Let's look at the biblical background on the mind. While the mind does not have one word that parallels to the English word. There are several Hebrew and Greek terms expressing your faculty of cognition in a comprehensible term. The King James Version offers six different Hebrew terms for mind: primary word "leb" meaning heart can be translated as mind (Num. 16:28, 1 Sam. 9:20, Neh. 4:6). And "nephesh" meaning soul can also be translated as mind *heart* (Deut. 18:6) referring to the desire of your mind/soul and (Gen. 23:8) refers to decision or judgment. Then there is "ruach" meaning spirit also translates as mind (Gen. 26:35) when it speaks of the grief of mind/spirit. Other words include "lebab" meaning heart (Ezek. 38:10), "yester" meaning imagination (Isa. 26:3) and "peh" meaning mouth, speech (Lev. 24:12).

The New Testament offers several terms describing our English word mind. Common terms are: nous & dianoia.

- Nous means seat of understanding, the place of knowing and reasoning, feeling and deciding.

- Dianoia referring to thinking through or thinking over resulting from reflection.

Other terms include kardia which means heart representing the concept mind. Ennoia meaning mind or intent. Gnome meaning purpose/opinion. Noema meaning thought process. Phronema meaning thought. Although the mind remains obscure, controversial and hard to define within the limits of our language we know that the mind is a result of brain activity. It's the key inherent characteristic of having life and a private place that only you can access; apart from God.

The mind is the center of your personality
The heart is the center of your being

Now physically, the heart is a key organ in the circulatory system that pumps blood throughout the vessels to various parts of the body. Each heartbeat, as repeated rhythmic contractions, transports oxygen and nutrients to every cell. The woman's heart is generally smaller than a man's heart simply because on average men are larger in overall body size. Outside of the physical, the heart has a wider meaning spiritually. This is where you need to follow closely. God looks at the heart, which is connected to both your mental and spiritual life and represents your true nature and character. The heart is where you understand and consider with wisdom things brought to your mind (Matt. 13:15). This is where you need to follow closely. The "inner heart" in scripture is ascribed to the fountain and seat of your *conduit* thoughts, passions, desires, affections, purposes, and appetite. It serves as the conduit for the will, feelings, and emotions to travel between your triune-being and throughout the various parts of the mind. Stay with me because this is important. The inner heart receives messages from the spirit to react and respond just as the physical heart receives messages from the body to pump more or less blood. It's these inner heart messages which stir-up intellect demanding a response. The response determines whether your connection is spiritual or physical. Without spiritual guidance, defilement (deceit/wickedness) hidden in the heart condemns you. You are told in Matthew 15:19 that, "...out of the heart comes "evil thoughts, murders, adulteries, fornications, thefts, false witness, blasphemies."

Reflection Moment: The inner heart reveals thoughts, passions, desires, affections, purposes, and appetite. What steps can you take to ensure your inner heart is pure before God?

-*misplaced emotions*-

It's important to address emotions again because emotions should never rule over you. They should not control your words, gestures, or feelings. Instead they should serve as an awareness to the body that a present experience or situation is stirring the senses. Emotions express strong feelings of love, anger, joy, hate, or fear. And so, it's important that your response comes from wisdom and restraint which is an indication of self-control. Positive emotions yield tolerant, creative, and expansive responses. Positive emotions also broaden the mind building and unifying the whole being; spirit, soul, and body. This reestablishes, increases, and strengthens your relationship with God because you're expanding beyond your own limited ability. But negative emotions narrow perspective to the point you only deal with the immediate threat(s). The focus becomes what's wrong which often leads to a loss of hope with no vision to see possibilities. Negative emotions produce withdrawal, disconnection, and a thrust into protection mode.

Emotions and feelings are two powerful sensations that can take you further than you intended to go and keep you longer than you intended to stay. Remember that. Ignoring feelings or deciding not to deal with them can be harmful in an experience because you've created the perfect storm. Unchecked negative emotions yield valley low experiences and cycles of confusion. However, choosing to correctly process anger is a sign of maturity. How is this accomplished? First, through understanding the need to postpone a response until self-control is present and balance is intact. This yields your triune being unto God for Him to "tag" those emotional data points that still need to be addressed or surrendered. Feelings and   *self-control* emotions should not be distractions that mislead or cause you to lash out on impulse. Bitterness and unforgiveness are two examples that harm self and others.

Yes, feelings and emotions are clearly provided for a reason. The Word of God tells you it's not wrong to be angry but sinning, or the response, can be wrong (Eph. 4:26-27). Your response is to be without sin. Therefore, it's important to use wisdom, restraint, and self-control in your daily walk and interactions. As women, we generally tend not to react on impulse as quickly as men, which reiterates the point that you can definitely exercise restraint over the mind. There may be a millisecond or second between thought and response. Whichever it is, it's enough time to choose the right response.

Emotions have their place but sin should not be the outcome

Being aware of thoughts is great, however, it's not enough. You need to really understand the power that a *Understand* thought has to becoming reality. Proverbs 23:7 says, "For as he thinketh in his heart, so is he." Thoughts can control the entire body directly or indirectly. How? As discussed with choices earlier, when you process a thought, it requires selecting from a multitude or series of ideas. Then that thought is provided with a skeletal framework, based on the idea, before it pulls in subsequent parts of memory, emotions, imagination, and will. Here, it's important to note that if your mind is God centered, your thoughts will reflect God. Isaiah 55:8-9 tells you that God's thoughts are not your thoughts nor His ways your ways. A God centered mind acknowledges God's claim over life and seeks to live in accordance with His will. This mind brings a wealth of power leading toward success and acts like a magnet attracting positivity from every angle influencing and impacting the thought process and response. Be a magnet. However, the ungodly mind is not centered and its thoughts reflect negativity and wickedness. This mind hinders you from hearing and seeing God, yielding thoughts to be de-moralizing and discouraging. It's your choice if you want your thought process to succeed or fail. With that being said, to some small extent you decide your destiny by the way you choose to think. In Romans 12:2 we are told, "Do not conform to the pattern of this world, but be transformed by the renewing of your mind. Then you will be able to test and approve what God's will is—his good, pleasing and perfect will."

*Being governed by spirit, you have access
to spiritual truths concerning the mind*

Meditation Point:

- Pay attention to your thoughts. Determine if they are positive or negative. Analyze your thought patterns. Ask yourself if this is a God inspired thought? Are my thoughts lining up with the Bible? Will this thought hinder my spiritual growth?
- Change or override negative persistent thought patterns (impure, unholy, filthy, unrighteous, and immoral) with positive thought patterns. Eliminate a negative thought with the Word of God and a positive thought. In Philippians 4:8 you are told, "Finally, brothers and sisters, whatever is true, whatever is noble, whatever is right, whatever is pure, whatever

is lovely, whatever is admirable—if anything is excellent or praiseworthy—think about such things."

- Celebrate accomplishments and the accomplishments of others by placing a positive thought on everything impacting you and others.

- Keep yourself surrounded by people who are likewise centered.

~~~

-compromised mind-

A breached mind is a compromised mind, which occurs when an infraction or violation occurs; this includes past situations or resurfaced experiences. This mind is an open gate for negative thoughts to enter as it tends to be "unkept" wandering constantly
wandering
and lacking control. Now, the mind itself is already said
to wander 30% of the time and as much as 70% when not extremely active. Therefore, if you don't have control of your mind, you are basically laying out a welcome mat for the enemy to walk on in. Whenever negativity lies dormant in the mind, it consumes your thoughts with disruptions that pop-up, blocking focus and god-centered thoughts. In Colossians 3:2, you are told to set your minds on things above not on earthly things. A compromised mind is in a cycle of entanglement "implanted" visual and mental images that violate the mind repeatedly. Note: An inward mind set eventually becomes an outward lifestyle, which in this case is harmful, non-productive, morally wrong,

injurious, and just in a disastrous state. There's a saying, "If you see dirt and play in dirt long enough, you'll eventually become dirty." A God centered mind responds to God's laws which gives life. In John 10:10 Jesus says, "I am come that they might have life, and that they might have it more abundantly." Abundance is happiness, peace, and gratification.

> The Holy Spirit, which dwells in the believer, is permanent but the anointing and power can depart based on the individual's choices. In the bible, David and Saul were kings that had a special anointing from God to be leaders over the people. But when Saul became wicked in the sight of the Lord, the Holy Spirit left Saul (1 Sam. 16:14) and he was "stuck" with an evil spirit. David, on the other hand, prayed not only to retain the indwelling of the Holy Spirit but the anointing to rule. Also, Samson (Judg. 16:20) had an anointing from God to lead Israel but because of his disobedience the Holy Spirit also left him.

The power of the Word of God is sharper than a double-edged sword, able to penetrate the soul and spirit discerning your thoughts and the intents of the heart (Heb. 4:12). Therefore, check every negative thought counteracting it with the Word of God. This is utilizing your authority! It's worth mentioning again, you have the right to refuse thoughts that try to infiltrate your mind. Otherwise, if you don't guard your thoughts you will gradually begin to decline in your character and increase excessively in your thoughts regarding self. These thoughts include self-advantages, pleasure, and well-being with little regard for others. Unguarded thoughts also tend to make you want to avoid inconvenience and discomfort. Therefore, if you willfully choose to remain in this sinful state, you are choosing to consider the things of God to be foolish and thus hostile toward God. This leads to spiritual death and lack of understanding for the gifts of God because they are spiritually discerned (1 Cor. 2:14). But receiving God brings you into a right relationship with Him along with the desire to do those things which please and honor Him. "Blessed are those who find wisdom, those who gain understanding" (Prov. 3:13).

Empty the self-filled mind and seek the godly-filled mind leading towards an empowered mind

⁓

-access-

In your human intellect you rely on understanding to perceive what is best but you are instructed in Proverbs 3:5 to trust in the Lord with all your heart and do not lean on or rely on your own understadning. Understanding derives from a word meaning "interval" or "space between" suggesting intellectual understanding involves the ability to pause or have a period of temporary cessation. It's in "the pause" where God provides discernment to recognize truth (life). Nevertheless, in our humanity (our understanding) we try to predict or anticipate what will happen next. When instead we should choose to fully put our trust in God with all of our heart and mind. Choosing to depend on God leads toward victory because God knows "the way to" and "the how to" of life. In every situation and circumstance, God will always provide a way of escape.

Be mindful of the real struggle which is in the constant tug-of-war between your two natures being spirit *tug-a-war* and flesh (old nature versus the new nature). In other words, you live and breathe in a body of flesh, but the real war is in the spirit and mind. You are battling against principalities, powers, and spiritual entities in high places. The enemy of God, satan, seeks to control your mind, alter your destiny, and destroy your soul. In Romans 7:23 it speaks about there being another law that lies within you warring against that law of your mind which seeks to bring you under the submission of sin. You must refuse to agree with a negative thought. Do not claim possession of, use, or take enjoyment of any opposing thought(s). Deny access! By refusing a negative thought the moment it arrives cuts that thought down. But much like a tree, you can cut it but the root may still be there. This means you may have to keep cutting the thought down until the root is removed. Victory is found in "Casting down imaginations, and every thing that exalteth itself against the knowledge of God, and bringing into captivity every thought to the obedience of Christ" (2 Cor. 10:5). Remove any thought or anything that tries to exalt itself above your pursuit of God. Often this means releasing negativity and past hurts that do not serve you well. Because God desires good for you. Note: Use your God given gift of discernment to determine the significance and worth of each choice set before you. Resist temptation (James 4:7) and drive away the enemy. Exercise restraint by taking authority and holding each thought to accountability, testing, and verifying it against The Word of God. This eliminates and prevents the spread of bad choices from flourishing.

Reflection Moment: Good news...you have the right to grant or deny thoughts permission to advance in the mind. What thoughts should you permit to remain?

Choices are the center of your ethical nature

-mind of God-

You have the ability to directly relate to the mind of God. The arduous part is setting aside the worlds system of knowledge and general laws. To access this ability, first and foremost ensure you're connected to the Holy Spirit. Again, this is being clothed with the Lord Jesus Christ (Rom. 13:14) under His authority, communing with Him. It's being covered to receive spiritual truth and perception into divine things to include recognizing good versus evil. Now, the beautiful covering of God unveils inner power to consider, judge soberly, and calmly within the gift of discernment, all representing your ability to relate to the mind of God. Being able to relate to God exemplifies the power of The Holy Spirit. In Philippians 2:8 Christ revealed His mind on the cross when He humbled Himself by becoming obedient to the point of death, even death on a cross. Christ, who chose to carry the cross, your sin, and old nature, ending the stronghold of darkness in your mind and all the miseries of arising sin, giving a way of escape through Him. With the stronghold of darkness removed you and I are able to live by the spirit. In Galatians 5:16-17 the Word says, "So I say, live by the Spirit, and you will not gratify the desires of the sinful nature. For the sinful nature desires what is contrary to the Spirit, and the Spirit what is contrary to the sinful nature." And Romans 7:23-25 says, "But I see another law in my members, warring against the law of my mind, and bringing me into captivity to the law of sin which is in my members. O wretched man that I am! Who will deliver me from this body of death? I thank God—through Jesus Christ our Lord!"

> Affirmations for the mind are a useful tool. It helps to keep what you affirm into the subconscious mind; keeping it a part of the subconscious mind consequently affecting your behavior and actions. Affirmations are a great tool and a positive assertion of what is in your mind and should solely be committed toward God. The response will be reflected in your life, behavior, choices, and actions all confirming you have a God centered mind.

The mind collects different aspects and processes them to reason in an attempt to discover what is true *steadfast* and what is best. The amazing power of choice comes with a responsibility to give careful thought to the paths you pick for your feet and to be steadfast in all our ways (Prov. 4:26). Because there is a way that appears right but ultimately leads to death (Prov. 14:12). Therefore, you need to be sure your mind is alert and fully sober. This means stay clear of things that could impair your decision making. For example, don't be drunk with wine which leads to reckless indiscretion instead make the choice to be filled with the Spirit (Eph 5:18). Don't be deceived into thinking your way is right apart from God. By now, you should understand the importance of guarding your mind from evil. The mind is a private place where only you should have the key.

Anchor your mind and be so secure that neither height nor depth can separate you from the love of God.

Change your thoughts
change your mind
And you change circumstances

Again, at the end of every thought there's a choice waiting for you to exercise judgment. Ask God to search your heart and thoughts and remove any offensive ways within (Ps. 139:23-24) so you can operate effectively as designed. And no matter the circumstances, with a made-up mind you determine how much a situation will affect you. Choose wisely. The path to a daily state of well-being and contentment is possible by doing the following:

- **Empty the mind daily.** Surrender to God and His spiritual truths; perceive divine things recognizing good and hating evil. Acknowledge God in His authority and right to reign over all creation both visible and invisible. Experience a relationship with God through studying and retaining His commandments, word, and promises in your heart and mind; by faith we understand these things.

- **Maintain power.** Bring your body to silence and be obedient to the Spirit until a separation from the natural into the spiritual occurs. Consider and judge soberly circumstances while keeping emotions and reactions under control. Focus all your thoughts on God's purpose, path, and thoughts toward you.

- **Labor for God.** Devote your time, gifts, and talents back to God. This brings complete peace with sincere devotion. Ensure your mind, will, heart, and understanding desire to delight God. Do this with determination and enthusiasm being ready, quick to act, and respond within your mind when making your choice.

If you need an example, look to the life of Christ, who prepared Himself to ultimately die for you. He was tormented for your salvation under circumstances that were meant to breakdown the human spirit and mind. And although you cannot compare your circumstances with Christ, you can look to Him as an example of a mind kept under severe circumstances. No matter what happens in this life you have the assurance of what is to come in the next life. You can make it through any and everything thrown your way if you keep Jesus as your central point of attention concentrating on His ways and commandments. Constantly bring your life back into focus by keeping your thoughts on the One who can keep you– God.

Reflection Moment: What are other things you should steer clear of that could impair your judgement?

-*nurture your spirit*-

The condition of your heart mirrors your relationship with The Father who is the Source of your power and strength. This produces the evidence of change and fruit of the spirit (Gal. 5:22-23). These fruits are:

Love – (in Greek "agape") referring to love that is given to others however, loving God is your primary obligation in life. Deuteronomy 6:4-6 commands you to "Love the Lord your God with all your heart and with all your soul and with all your strength. These commandments that I give you today are to be on your hearts." And then love is said to be the fulfillment of the law in Galatians 5:14, "Love your neighbor as yourself."

Joy - related to grace which is an expression of thankfulness to God for forgiveness and acceptance. An inward sense of joy, despite circumstances, is a characteristic point of the grace of God.

Peace – more than the absence of strife. It's wholeness, health, and balance. Peace describes your relationship, as a believer, to God in light of the cross.

Longsuffering - (in Greek "makrothumia") means great sacrifice. It's patient and slow to anger.

Kindness - similar to generosity (in Greek "krestotes") expressed in mildness and kindness toward others. Kindness is having a generous heart or to offer a donation from the heart by free-will.

Goodness - refers to acts of love, or lovingkindness, regarded as good in the eyes of God. Goodness is the practice of love regarded greater than just doing the right thing out of a sense of duty; it's compassion.

Faithfulness – connected to integrity of the heart which brings about a sense of trustworthiness in a person. Faithfulness is related with truth implying trust-worthiness, reliability, etc.

Humility - implies a sense of inner poverty only healed by giving and serving others. Humility indicates courtesy focusing on honoring and esteeming others better than yourself.

Modesty - an inner strength that refers to the power of the Holy Spirit residing in you. Modesty is the strength by God to choose the good; putting away the flesh.

You can either sow to the flesh and reap corruption or you can sow to the Spirit and reap life everlasting (Gal. 6:7-8). Exercising your faith is important because the end result will be a nurtured spirit and con-nected heart to God that will produce the fruit of righteousness. Note:

The flesh will resist and lament over such exercise. This is where you push the body into submission of the spirit.

Nurturing your spirit is key to life. Therefore, understanding the spiritual realm and its accessibility, as a believer, allows you to enter the place that unveils the secret places to where God is. This is amazing. God will lead you to and put you in places where He (Life) dwells. Peace will be found in these places not strife. You live in Him and He in you for He has given you His Spirit (1 John 4:13). Nurturing your spirit allows you to visualize and ultimately reach your destiny not in your own strength but in God's strength and power. This takes self-discipline which once achieved allows others to witness God changing and working in your life. Note: Through the Holy Spirit you know God's will and follow His decrees. Simply ask God to reveal to you His spiritual truths that you may obey them. And then wait for the answer. He guarantees you will receive an answer.

Be present seeing everything with clear vision. Look at situations going from here forward knowing that God is on your side and you will receive deliverance, victory, and prosperity. Be of one mind and one soul (Phil. 1:27). Be not wise in your own eyes but fear the Lord and keep away from evil. This brings health to your body and nourishment to the bones (Prov. 3:7-8). Look to Christ who exemplified the mind you ought to have as He focused on those things concerning the kingdom and glorifying The Father in heaven. Know who you're really trying to impress – God. Love God with all of your mind (Matt. 22:37). And know that the problem is not with the mind itself but rather the misuse of the mind. A person who does not accept the things of the Spirit cannot access the full potential of the mind or spirit because this comes from the Spirit of God. That's super important! You are not designed to live life aimlessly, you are designed to live life with a purpose and make choices that stem from your spiritual perception, introspection, memory, creativity, imagination, conceptions, belief, reasoning, volition, and emotions. Will you be perfect? Absolutely not. But when properly aligned at least you're aiming for perfection. And you will experience the fuller things of God. In closing remember, if you want to be great you need to learn to be a servant, which starts with letting nothing be done through strife or vain glory (wrong motives), but rather in lowliness of mind esteeming others over yourself (Phil. 2:3).

Reflection Moment: What have you learned about the mind that you didn't know before?

-five-

soul

soul

| **soul** |

designates life
inseparable part of our being
supports both spiritual and physical strength

The first proof of loyalty to God was planted in the midst of the Garden of Eden, known as the tree of life. This tree symbolized access to eternal life and eating from the tree brought knowledge of good and evil. If you know the story…after Adam and Eve disobeyed God's command, the consequence of sin not only interrupted their quality of life, God intended, but their relationship also with God changed. One significant change was that they no longer had access to the tree of life. Wait, what! Not having direct access to life is huge! But Jesus, who is Life, took upon Himself our sin and made the ultimate sacrifice giving up His life on the cross (tree) so that we could gain access again to eternal life through Him. Hallelujah! Understanding that life comes from God and only God can sustain life should be enough to make you want to remain connected. Adam and Eve's bad decision/choice is a reminder, or lesson learned, to be careful of what you allow yourself to hear, see, and receive so that you don't drift away from God. Drifting is a slow process that gradually takes you away from true life, diminishing hope, making you numb to the world, and eventually causing spiritual death. Pay attention to the caution signs. If you begin to feel any of those things just mentioned, here are a few things you can do: First, stop and acknowledge God in all your ways and He will direct your path (Prov. 3:6). Secondly, drop distractions and attentively listen for the call of God (through silence) who loves you and desires only good for you. And finally, roll into diligent and persistent spiritual warfare mode pressing into the presence of God to know Him, His love, and His will. Arm yourself with the Word of God ready to fight. Seek, find, and be filled (Matt. 5:6).

> God is the giver of all life both physically and mentally. From the dust of the earth, which man was formed, God imparted His divine Spirit (breath). Life is having ownership or occupancy of a soul in which mankind displayed after receiving God's breath (Spirit). Throughout the Bible God's consistent theme of change and transformation is revealed in scripture. Transformation comes when you recognize God seeking His direction.

A refined mind is a pure soul

The **Soul** Soul *Soul* designates physical and spiritual life. It's vitality in all its breadth and width and the force that animates our innermost will and desires. You're a living soul with the power *vitality* to live, grow, and have a meaningful purposed journey. The soul, like a mirror, reflects your thought process and heart illuminating areas aligned or misaligned with God. And when you lift your soul up to God you are: 1) redirecting your will to consciously focus on God and choosing to trust in Him and His word; 2) cleaning areas to realign with God which refines your reasoning and thought process through purification and separation from earthly matters, detaching self from sin; 3) increasing purity which should be your desire. Guard your life by keeping the commandments of The Lord. Note: again remember, often times under pressure, the weakness of mankind has been to revert back to what is familiar instead of choosing to lift the soul up to God and righteousness. Resist sin and desire to be holy as God is holy. A person who is heedless of their ways and unconcerned about the call to obedience is misaligned with error which results in death (Prov. 14:12). An example and lesson to learn from are the Israelites. Their thoughts were illuminated (soul) as they wandered in the desert for way too long complaining and murmuring misaligned instead of trusting God moving forward into the promise land.

The soul acts as a "bridge" to the spirit and body *bridge* providing passage to the heart uniting the triune being. This is where you need to follow closely. Because as you encounter experiences, they pass through the soul (i.e. feelings, wishes, will, etc.) which is where you then designate or choose the action that should be applied. In other words, the soul "marks or tags" each encountered experience placing it toward reason and purpose. But it's an intersection where choice meets action and decisions meet success or failure. If you didn't understand that, go back and reread it because it's important to catch. At this intersection, the question becomes will you be obedient or disobedient to the voice and commands of God? It's worth taking a moment, or more, at this juncture (pause) to be completely sure your soul (innermost will and desires) is surrendered unto God. When you let go of the control, you actually gain control. It's true God will fight for you. But you first must become weak and surrender to Him. For God is our refuge and strength ever present in times of trouble (Ps. 46:1). And all things work together for good (Rom. 8:28).

-aware-

The spirit is God aware, soul is self- aware, and the body is world aware. Each inseparable part makes a whole, complete, and perfect you. Regarding soul self-awareness it's having knowledge and *knowledge* consciousness to receive ideas, suggestions, offers, and admission. It's also being aware of sensations, thoughts, surroundings, etc. Beyond self-awareness, especially for women, God provided "mankind awareness". Meaning, whatever you receive is brought together with a commitment to hold, bear, and deliver a final product. You bring it all together to work together! Note: through the soul you are affected and influenced making it also a place often attacked. The enemy is constantly targeting the soul to control your mental and emotional sensibility. Therefore, the soul too needs to be kept, renewed, preserved, and protected which is accomplished by not allowing world awareness (body) to rule over God awareness (spirit). This includes not allowing the mind to rehash past hurts but instead choosing forgiveness and peace in its place. In Philippians 3:12, you are told to forget those things which are behind and reach for those things that are ahead. Keep God as your focus. Only then, will you find you're no longer moved by external circumstances but instead live, move, and have your being securely grounded in the truth of God's unfailing love.

The soul sets you apart from inanimate objects

Being richly filled with life is grasping the realm of the sacred, being grateful for life, and recognizing the reason for your existence. You serve the One who sent His son Jesus *grateful* so that you may have life abundantly (John 10:10). Life is the core of who you are. That's worth reading again. Beyond the day-to-day routine God wants to break the chains of the old way of doing things, release bad habits, and open the doors to divine life. So much so that God dispatches His angels to help you and breaks darkness to bring you out of lack into abundance. By recognizing your own biases and lack of knowledge, you become humble and ready to receive wisdom. Wisdom transforms your way of thinking so you can succeed. Success and joy come from living in accordance with the orderliness God has placed in the world. Life is more than being rewarded by this world or relying on your own self-sufficiency. Life is gaining wisdom from God (Prov. 2:6). Understand that the soul is where you refine your reasoning and thought process. And it's where life is confirmed as a gift from God. Note: you will not be able to rationalize or blame others for not choosing abundant life because of the power of choice.

A call to worship is an awareness of the profane sacred (holy) space God fills within you, the universe, and the earth. You are instructed to worship God in spirit and in truth (John 4:24). This is where you connect to The Source of Life receiving nourishment and provided with strength and power to live supporting your existence. It didn't say to worship God in body and in truth but to worship in spirit and in truth. For God Is a Spirit. The union of our spirit brings forth the fruits of the spirit (love, joy, peace, meekness, etc.) within you.

Deep things of God call to the deep things within the spirit. Without a doubt, God is constantly drawing you closer to Himself and purpose. However, don't forget there's a constant attempt to derail, confuse, and distract you away from God and purpose. Thus, there's no room for the soul to be broken, imbalanced, insecure, vulnerable, or weak to tactics that come to kill, steal, and destroy. That's why it's so important to constantly perform self-check awareness to confirm who's at the center of your heart and decision making. If it's you at the center, you're guaranteed eventual emptiness and frustration. You cannot serve two masters; cannot have two kings. But if it's God at the center, you will be complete, aligned, and filled. But be ready for resistance. It's not an easy given pass, you've got to put some work into maintaining your place and connection with God. Perhaps this isn't emphasized enough. I'll repeat it again... living a godly life is work. But living an ungodly life is work too with no good reward in the end. Therefore, daily or even hourly, if necessary, purge your soul from carnal or evil desires replacing them with holy affections. Because this is the way forward to true life. Serve God in your soul (mind) where you profit, produce, and receive the surplus of God. If you remember your instructions to love the Lord your God with all of your heart and with all of your mind (Mark 12:30) you're guaranteed abundant life.

~~~

-spiritual warfare-

At times in war there is shrapnel or shell fragments that cause life-changing injuries and even kill. And in certain circumstances, doctors may leave those foreign objects in the body because they are unreachable. Thus, the body heals with these foreign objects by walling them off with inflammation and forming tissue around it. And then, after some time, it may be easier to remove with surgery, but the concern remains, the pieces of these foreign objects could move and shift making it difficult to find and remove. Now, apply this same concept to spiritual warfare, first understand there is a constant spiritual warfare occurring in the universe and around you. And at times, shrapnel hits the spirit and soul causing injuries. These shrapnel fragments may otherwise be known as abuse, fear, loneliness, isolation, resentment, etc. which were never intended for your life, however, you still got hit. The good news is that you have also been given the power to be victorious over such afflictions. Afflictions cause pain, distress, and misery, both mentally and physically, but they don't have to pierce through the soul which remember designates physical and spiritual life. Such fragments are reachable by The Great Physician, God, so that you don't have to build up walls around shrapnel or shell fragments. They don't have to travel to the heart or cause spiritual death. In I Peter 5:8, you are instructed to be alert and of sober mind for your enemy, the devil, prowls like a roaring lion looking for someone to destroy. Like a "roaring lion" is not the same as a roaring lion. Jesus is the Lion of Judah who triumphed over temptation and sin, pain and suffering, fear and death. In 2 Corinthians10:3-5 says, "For though we walk in the flesh, we do not war after the flesh: For the weapons of our warfare are not carnal, but mighty through God to the pulling down of strong holds. Casting down imaginations, and every high thing that exalteth itself against the knowledge of God, and bringing into captivity every thought to the obedience of Christ."

Spiritual warfare attacks both the mind and judgement. The after-effects may not be easy to describe however, they are felt in moments of depression, discouragement, agitation, etc. that seem to "pop-up" or appear out of nowhere. And just knowing there is a war being waged over your soul and mind is an indication that you shouldn't shrug off rainy day blues as nothing, but instead get into your warfare position. Withstanding spiritual attacks causes the enemy to flee from you (James 4:7). It's worth mentioning again that the authority and power you've received through Jesus Christ is more than enough to be victorious over the enemy. There's no need to lay low and suffer while being attacked. Use your spiritual weapons described in Ephesians 6, "Put on the whole armour of God, that ye may be able to stand against the wiles of the devil. For we wrestle not against flesh and blood, but against princi-palities, against powers, against the rulers of the darkness of this world, against spiritual wickedness in high places. Wherefore take unto you the whole armour of God, that ye may be able to withstand in the evil day, and having done all, to stand. Stand therefore, having your loins girt about with truth, and having on the breastplate of righteousness; And your feet shod with the preparation of the gospel of peace; Above all, taking the shield of faith, wherewith ye shall be able to quench all the fiery darts of the wicked. And take the helmet of salvation, and the sword of the Spirit, which is the word of God: Praying always with all prayer and supplication in the Spirit, and watching thereunto with all perseverance and supplication for all saints."

You're commanded to "fear not". Why? Because a heart of fear expresses sin which is practicing the absence of God instead of practicing His presence. The only fear you should have is the fear (reverence) toward God. For God's love casts out fear which torments you (1 John 4:18). God has not given you a spirit *reverence* of fear but of power, love, and a sound mind (2 Tim. 1:7). The Greek word for "sound mind" means safe. Again, every woman wants to feel safe. You are never alone. In Isaiah 43 you are told that, "When you pass through the waters, I will be with you; and when you pass through the rivers, they will not sweep over you. When you walk through the fire, you will not be burned; the flames will not set you ablaze." God sees and understands your struggles. Turn and run toward the open arms of God receiving His love. Jeremiah 29:11 says, "For I know the thoughts that I think toward you, saith the Lord, thoughts of peace, and not of evil, to give you an expected end." You will never be led to a place where His love will not be there.

By now, you should know your complaint or chief informant is satan. He is the continuous relentless accuser of God's children. Recognizing there is a demonic force that opposes and attacks you means you also recognize the importance of knowing and speaking forth The Word of God to combat the enemy. Follow closely as we look to the life of Jesus who used several ways to handle His accusers. One way was by remaining silent before them. Note: I believe in these moments Jesus was communing with the Father. Jesus always had the cross before His eyes and completed His mission being crucified. Jesus didn't respond to the evil men who brought Him before Pontius Pilate nor did He seek to change Pilate's mind by arguing with the accusers. Jesus remained silent, as the prophets foretold, being the Lamb of God sacrificed to redeem a people for Himself. Scriptures to meditate on concerning spiritual warfare are: James 4:7 says, "Submit yourselves, then, to God. Resist the devil, and he will flee from you." In 1 Peter 5:8 we are told, "Be alert and of sober mind. Your enemy the devil prowls around like a roaring lion looking for someone to devour." John 8:32 says, "And you shall know the truth, and the truth shall make you free." Romans 8:1-39 says, "Therefore, there is now no condemnation for those who are in Christ Jesus. For in Christ Jesus the law of the Spirit of life set you free from the law of sin and death..." Luke 10:19 says, "I have given you authority to trample on snakes and scorpions and to overcome all the power of the enemy; nothing will harm you." Romans 12:19 says, "Do not take revenge, my dear friends, but leave room for God's wrath, for it is written: "It is mine to avenge; I will repay," says the Lord." And your response should be great joy knowing Christ died for you; setting you free. You ought to live for His glory placing your trust in Christ alone for salvation.

Reflection Moment: Isaiah 54:17 says, that no weapon formed against you will prosper. List ways you will guard your soul to win the battle of the mind.

True life and purpose involve having the mind of Christ

Pull down strongholds. Pull down lies stunting your spiritual growth. Resist strongholds in your attitude, emotions, and behavior. Allow God to heal every traumatic event still affecting your life. This moves you out of "survival mode" to the path of true life. In Psalms 9:9 you are told that, "The Lord is a refuge for the oppressed, a stronghold in times of trouble." While it's the enemy's job is to get you to challenge or question God and His Word... it's your job to rebuke the constant attempts of the enemy to plant thoughts or imaginations in   *rebuke* the mind that are contrary to the will of God. A carnal mind brings corruption leading to spiritual death. However, victory comes when your eyes see The Word of God and your spirit receives the Word, which protects and guards the soul. A God centered mind brings life, joy, and peace. In Matthew 6:22-23 it says, "The light of the body is the eye: if therefore thine eye be single, thy whole body shall be full of light. But if thine eye be evil, thy whole   *righteously* body shall be full of darkness. If therefore the light that is in thee be darkness, how great is that darkness!"

God is the center of all existence and all life

Paul, in the Bible, tells you that there is a war within you. That the flesh craves what is contrary to the spirit and the spirit what is contrary to the flesh. It's important reiterate the need to check the "old self" (flesh) to ensure it's not in control or attempting to dethrone your soul. Romans, chapter 7, describes the struggle with sin further

"… that which I do, I would not, and that which I would not, I do. O, wretched man that I am, who shall deliver me from this body of death". We've all experienced weakness of the flesh. We say we'll do things and… we don't do them. And those things we say I will never do again… we do them again. There is an escape from the bondage of the flesh! Sin doesn't have to rule your life because you are no longer under the law but rather under grace. Be steadfast and determined to remain in the will of God which enables you to make good decisions and judgment. The mind and emotions can betray you, but the spirit will not. Nothing satan offers will bring true life because he is NOT the giver of life. God will mend the broken pieces within, as only He can, in the most beautiful way.

Meditation Point:

In Isaiah chapter 53 it reads, "We all, like sheep, have gone astray, each of us has turned to our own way; and the LORD has laid on him the iniquity of us all" which indicates that your sins fell on Jesus as He made intercession for you (Isa. 53:12). A war occurred between the powers of hell and Jesus at the cross. Jesus defeated the enemy and won. Today, Jesus intercedes for you at the right hand of the Father.

∽

-life in the soul-

The soul serves you in several ways: 1) designating feelings, wishes, and will; 2) holding negative and positive emotions; emphasizing will-power; and 3) labeling true life. Consider, if you will, the heart for a moment. The heart pumps blood throughout the body to all the organs and tissue that need oxygen and nutrients. You are alive based off the organ's function, demonstrating reception of blood. Likewise, the soul seeks and pumps true life in your thought process, supporting both spirit and body. Now, the soul accurately points to areas labeling where life (God) dwells in feelings, emotions, wishes, dreams, will, and purpose. This reflection of life shows *accurately* your reception of God in the mind and will. And a proper connection brings forth clarity which is seen in your decisions and reactions. John 13:35 says, "By this everyone will know that you are my disciples, if you love one another." Love, which is of God, does not walk in the counsel of the ungodly, nor stand among sinners, nor sit in the seat of the scornful, but rather delights in the law of the Lord and those who meditate day and night. This is the place where you will be planted by streams of water (life) finding inner peace, quietness of the soul, tranquility, and peace within the heart.

The soul makes you a complete individual

The Bible is filled with imperfect people who had one thing going for them...they were after God's heart. This made the difference! Being after God's heart brings forth true repentance and change. It's again following the commandment found in Deuteronomy 6:4 that you are to love the Lord thy God with all your heart and soul (mind). An example of love is David, who poured his soul (heart) out before the Lord as a sacrifice without caring what others thought of him because he understood the key to obtain and maintain true life. Offering and surrendering your feelings, wishes, and will (soul) to God ignites something wonderful and supernatural within. Another example are the women at the tomb of Lazarus, who poured their souls out through weeping at the devastation of the death of Lazarus. It was their raw emotions touched the heart of Jesus who also wept demonstrating His understanding of your soul. Through these examples, you learn to empty the soul before God for answers, healing, reignition, refreshment, and revival. In Psalms 19:7 you are told, "The law of the Lord is perfect, refreshing the soul. The statutes of the Lord are trustworthy, making wise the simple." In addition, God requires a measure of your faith. Faith is also a fruit of the Spirit (Gal. 5:22). Just think of the great things you will accomplish with a made-up mind towards God. You will move mountains! In 1 Corinthians 2:6-16, Paul speaks of God's power revealed to those having the mind of Christ; not by the wisdom of the world. Therefore, let God be the reflection seen in your heart and response. Be after God's heart!

Finally, the soul craves and seeks life. However, be sure you're following and rendering yourself to God and not the world because there are false gods in this world that mankind has tried to replace God with; even making themselves a god. There is a way that appears to be right, but the end leads to death and destruction (Prov. 14:12). Refuse ungodly and negative opposing forces, denying access or permission to anything contrary to the Word of God. Don't allow anything not of God to take root and grow in your soul. Note: the soul is designed to operate without disruption, so if you experience emotions of being overwhelmed, lost, confused, hopeless, depressed, fearful, angry, or even suicidal, you're under a spiritual attack. You are designed to live by the Word of God and His commandments.

The soul is an intimate and inseparable part of your triune being

Reflection Moment: As God equips you to serve Him, what can you do to help/serve others?

-soul health-

Recall that a healthy soul functions as a "bridge" between: 1) the breath of God (spirit) living in you; and 2) the body (flesh). So, if the soul is restless it will not be able to operate as the spanning structure that it's designed to be providing passage to life. Make it your prayer to fully experience God, in all of His beauty, and come into the understanding of true life because in this your soul will prosper and be healthy. In this your soul will be sound, even in the midst of a storm, and you will have a vigorous mind. In Matthew 16:26 it says, "For what should it profit a man, if he would gain the whole world, and lose his own soul?" This world's "stuff" gets *eternal* old fast! Real joy is in eternal things that cross over the line of death with you (John 10:27-28). A relationship with God, mankind, service to others, exemplifying love, and the use of your talents to honor and glorify God are eternal. Here you profit! It's worth more than anything the world can offer.

We are but strangers passing through this world

A healthy soul points out areas NOT properly aligned and areas where life has ceased. You don't just want to pass over these areas but remove them. Note: this includes toxic relationships. Let's just clarify there is nothing wrong with distancing yourself from toxic people in order to maintain a healthy soul. I call this practice "soul protection" which doesn't make you a bad person. It's not wrong to pray for folks from a safe distance. Now, with that being said, as the soul is in a constant effort to bridge between spirit and body it continuously offers up clarity leading towards true life, but again the choice is yours. Let's review core needs to be healthy. They are: 1) spirit needs to be connected to God and nurtured by Him; 2) soul needs to be regulated, supported, and balanced; and 3) body needs to eat, drink, be clothed, and under subjection of the spirit. When core needs are not met, derailment occurs. And derailment is chaos found in dysfunction, abuse (physical and emotional), addictions, and an overall misuse of life. Do you have any derailments in your life? The enemy often uses these tactics in hopes of reducing or delaying the chances for your success and development. Yes, the enemy is busy, but with God nothing can hinder or cause you to become deflected from purpose. There is no failure in God.

The soul represents your capacity to survive and live a meaningful life. What does a healthy soul look like? A healthy soul is grounded, steadfast, immovable, always abounding in the work of the Lord (1 Cor. 15:58) designating areas where life (God) resides. As you follow God, you are following light. Not the physical entity that we call light but the first form of light – God. God Himself is light (Ps. 27:1). And God's Word is light to your path (Ps. 119:195). God, who is light, eliminates darkness silencing distractions. Do not be like some who love darkness better than light because of their evil lifestyle, obscurity, and actions. Instead, walk in The Light where understanding and purity (righteousness) are found. By following the commandments of God which regulate your life, you're ensuring accuracy, operation, and order are correct within your triune being. It is God who brings balance while the enemy often uses the things of the world to bring distractions, misalignment, and disconnection. Following God, who covered Himself in light, will guide you, help you to process, and break down experiences with mental clarity. He will move you towards victory and a successful journey. Note: the flip side, spiritual death, is when the body is allowed to lead bringing stagnation with no movement and without progression. With the body leading, the body seeks only to satisfy the needs of the body which is NOT the will of God.

> Nephesh meaning life or possessing life carries a similar meaning in the New Testament psuche. God, who breathed nephesh or life into the dust of the earth (Gen 2:7) in which you in turn, carry a portion of His Spirit within; thus, a soul. The soul refers to the inner part of a person and even represents the person as a whole. The soul 1) reflects the condition and stage of the individual concerning God; and 2) exhibits the condition of the mind.

If you don't value life it's possible to easily lose your soul

With a broken soul you're not functioning as you should, at full capability, because you're built to prosper. In 3 John 1:2 it says, "Beloved, I wish above all things that thou mayest prosper and be in health, even as thy soul prospereth." There's a clear relationship between prosperity of the physical well-being and the soul. Even the medical field sees the correlation between mental health and physical health. For example, if you have a bad attitude this creates bad chemicals that attack and harm the body lowering your defense to maintain good health. But how can you prosper with a broken soul that indicates there's discontent? The fix is found in Matthew 6:33, "Seek the Kingdom of God above all else, and live righteously, and he will give you everything you need." For you are called to walk in truth not conflict, so get rid of all the filth and evil in your lives, and humbly accept The Word God has planted in your hearts, for it has the power to save your soul (James 1:21). Many times, your issues have nothing to do with the physical body but rather the condition of the soul. The scripture goes on to say that you are deceiving yourself if you only be a hearer of the Word but not a doer.

Don't allow negative emotions to deteriorate your soul

Finally, rest is good for the soul. On the seventh day God rested (Gen. 2:3) and presented a timeline or pattern as an example to show you the blessing of rest. Rest is required and necessary to hear God (silence). So, if you ever needed permission to stop and step away to digest the beauty of God's creative works, here's your pass! Stop and smell the flowers, take in the beauty of the fields draped with color and be grateful. Marvel at the smallest ant and the highest mountain. Yes, marvelous are the works of God! Observe a day of rest. Without it the soul will be incited, embittered, unsettled, or kept in suspense. However, with rest you will be able to focus on the glass being half full, enlarging your outlook on life's experiences. Rest will make you strong, flourish, and prosper. Note: in the New Testament, the soul and spirit are spoken of interchangeably and distinguished different from the body.

Reflection Moment: God desires you have peace (Jer. 29:11). What areas do you still need peace in?

∽

-response-

How you answer God is everything because your
answer
answer can bring life together in such a wonderful way to
where you see the hidden beauty, worth, and value in life again. Let
your answer be one of obedience. In the Bible, you can read about many
strong women who obeyed God, even breaking tradition in order to do
the right thing. Mary accepted her calling to carry and birth the savior
of the world. Shiphrah and Puah, in the book of Exodus, feared God
more than the king of Egypt and decided not to follow the command
to kill all the Hebrew boys when they were born, but instead they did
what was right in the eyes of God. Rahab, a prostitute, recognized and
feared the God of the Israelite spies and protected them instead of
handing them over to the King of Jericho. Lydia, worshipper of God
and businesswoman, received baptism as one of the first converts to
Christianity along with her entire household, and then opened her
house to Paul and the missionaries. Ruth followed Naomi to Israel
devoting herself to the Lord playing a significant role in the coming of
Jesus. Mary Magdalene was healed by Jesus and then joined His ministry
later to be the first witness of the empty tomb of Christ. And so many
more women responded to God's call on their heart.

Being able to love comes by way of the miracle of God (Ezek.
36:26). Walking with God enables you to find life, love, truth, and
salvation. And the greatest response you can have toward God is love.
It's the love of Christ that constrains you (2 Cor. 5:14). The Spirit

searches all things even the deep things of God. Thus, by silencing the physical wandering mind and opening up your spirit to God, you become connected, and the mind is then made searchable, cleansed, and freed from worldly pollutants that were permitted to enter (consciously or subconsciously). That's worth reading again. God supersedes all your understanding so without the Spirit of God you cannot accept the things of God. Now, this may be the arduous part but if you desire to walk in the spirit of truth, you will not allow the mind to wander aimlessly. Instead welcome the Spirit of God to teach you and receive spiritual truths that will help you in all things.

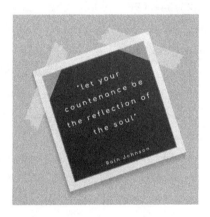

All things work together for the good of them that love God (Rom. 8:28). As you love God everything starts cohesively working together. You'll want to receive from God which allows you to not only hear and process experiences of life but also be able to answer in accordance with truth, even in times of emotional turmoil. Ture, life is not always fair but God is. God is just, good, and holy whether others are not or even you yourself are not. Keep speaking life to yourself and others focusing on areas where life resides. Do not apply life to a lifeless situation where God does not want you to be. Move forward. In Proverbs 18:21 it says, "The tongue has the power of life and death, and those who love it will eat its fruit." Respond to life's situations with faith. Faith cometh by hearing and hearing by the Word of God (Rom. 10:17). Love God with all of your soul (Mark 12:30) with all of your emotions and mind. Through love you connect to hope. Paul, in the Bible, writes about the hope of sharing the glory of God and declared that this hope does not disappoint as your hearts have been filled with God's love through the Holy Spirit.

The Hebrew word for soul is nephesh which means throat; refers to the hungry, thirsty, satisfied, soul. The function of the throat stands for the human desire and longing you have for God. It also can stand for the human desire and longing mankind has after power, sex, satisfaction, and even evil. Understanding the soul helps you to control and balance your life. Now, the Greek word psyche refers to the ideas of body, flesh and spirit to characterize human existence.

Emotions allow you to bond and connect with God & others

Reflection Moment: You are created perfectly. God did not give you low self-esteem or confidence issues. Take a moment and list all of your positive attributes.

-connection-

In John 15:4-5 Jesus says, "Live in me and I will live in you". This is basically the carnal nature being replaced with a radically brand-new nature based on the Spirit and resurrection life. Yes, it's a miracle found in the connection with Jesus' life. The scripture then goes on to say, "as the branch cannot bear fruit by itself, unless it finds life in the vine, neither can you, unless you find life in me; for apart from me you can do nothing". Thus, you cannot bring forth any worthwhile fruit to God without the indwelling of the power of Jesus Christ. Anything you do for God apart from Jesus Christ is barren. Let the carnal nature be put on the cross as you join yourself with His death, burial, and resurrection; death-for-death and life-for-life. This is in the profession by faith and the truth about who you are as written in Galatians 2:20. I have been crucified with Christ and am no longer I who live but Christ who lives in me. Connecting to the source of life brings joy, strength, and nourishment needed to truly live. It clothes you in righteousness accepting His redeeming love for your life. Note: be mindful not to pray for God to have mercy and grace on that which should be crucified with Christ.

Your beautiful bond with God and mankind includes sensitivity. Sensitivity is another strength, not a weakness. *sensitivity* You are endowed with the operation and function of the senses which elevate your perception and awareness. Being sensitive increases your mental condition and physical feelings. And as you receive, you are quickened to action, feeling, and thought all as a part of being sensitive to both internal and external change. Yes, these are all useful and desirable qualities serving you and mankind as a resource. Being in constant stillness and communion with God mitigates external worldly influences. Also, remaining connected ensures the health of your mental and emotional state. Let me add, being sensitive is the awareness of and responsiveness to the feelings of others, but this may mean that you often put yourself on the back burner to ensure others are taken care of first. Therefore, remember to conduct a self-check to ensure balance. Being out of balance causes easy irritation, annoyance, and means you're pouring too much from one part of your triune being. Note: the soul guides you to truth as God is truth. Another advantage to sensitivity is that The Spirit of God will help you speak and react to experiences/situations correctly. Finally, the key thing to understand about sensitivity is that it elevates spiritual perception and awareness which takes you quickly into the presence of God; the heartbeat of God. This safe place is where you pour yourself out. It's where you find refreshment, renewal, rejuvenation, revival, and release from everything concerning/worrying you. And this place is where God can sort through all the "muck" laying in the soul restoring you back to the right place and perspective of life.

As women, we share a common connection that bonds us together beyond culture or background. We share traits, qualities, and features that characterize us as woman. This DNA was formed in the beginning through creation. Accept and connect with your inherent power and strength to transform into the woman that the world needs. Times are changing and we are rapidly moving from managing the home and being detached from the corporate world to now pursuing education and thinking independently along with male counterparts. You do not have to behave more like a man nor be tougher. Discrimination on the basis of gender is diminishing and women are recognized as an important contributor to society. The challenge now is managing both spheres of home life and a career. We face emotional struggles of leaving children in day care or school to pursue our careers. And some have even decided to give up on having a family to pursue their goals only to ask themselves later if the career really made them feel successful. Rely on your spiritual connection for strength, security, balance, and wisdom.

Women are strong supporters. In a relationship when we are not able to meet the needs of another, we often allow self-blame, sadness, or self-doubt to set in. Women are twice as likely to suffer from depression than men according to the CDC, and this spans across all racial, ethnic, and economic divides. Don't allow yourself to be in bondage emotionally. Set boundaries for yourself that will not receive lies that make you doubt yourself. Choose to only receive truth. Believe God and not what others say about you. If you believe negative things about yourself, you project negativity. Therefore, remove all negativity because you're too valuable. Don't let negativity be a tool of control to keep you feeling worthless. The truth is that you were born into a world that has enough space for you and your gifts, and you belong in every area of life. The truth is that you compliment mankind in every way, both intellectually and spiritually. You established unity of the human race guaranteeing your dignity and worth, and anyone who has a problem with this should take it up with God. Because God deemed man incomplete by himself.

You yield different results when you "walk in truth"

Evidence of the Spirit of God working in you will be love, joy, peace, patience kindness, goodness, faithfulness, gentleness, and self-control (Gal. 5:22-23). Maintain your fervor, enthusiasm and zeal for God without worry about those who kill the body but instead fear Him (God) who is able to destroy both soul and body in hell (Matt. 10:28).

Reflection Moment: I find it interesting that an elephant, one of the smartest, largest animals on the planet, when in captivity and restrained long enough, over time breaks down and accepts they are not free. Even if untied and freed, the elephant continues to live as if captive and restrained within the boundaries that were set. Is there anything holding you captive even though God has freed you?

-six-

identification

identification

| i•den•ti•fi•ca•tion |

perception of another as an extension of oneself
condition or character as to who a person is;
qualities, beliefs, etc.sense of self, providing
sameness and continuity in personality
over time exact likeness; in nature or qualities

T he world has numerous methods and technologies to identify people individually and uniquely with documents like birth certificates, driver's license, social security cards, passports, etc.

And then there's fingerprints which use our unique *unique* epidermis ridges and furrows (valleys) on our fingertips which seem to be the most reliable personal identification tool. But looking back to the beginning, God clearly provided each of us with unique purpose along with a personal relationship with Him. Identity is key because how you identify yourself is what you will model in your thoughts, feelings, and actions. And while the world's methods of ID are not intrinsically bad, they should not be the source of your identity as a child of God. Check and be sure you have not adapted to the world's systematic belief of who you are. Identification (ID) should be looked at with supernatural and spiritual lenses which requires being in-agreement with God's description, naming, and recognition of who you are. This is understanding your value and existence.

There are so many examples in the Bible of women and men who were reminded of who they were created to be. For example, an angel appeared unto Mary and said to her, "Greetings, you who are highly favored! The Lord is with you" (Luke 1:28). Mary was reminded that she was highly favored and that the Lord is with her! Sarah was reminded that she is not barren but a mother who would receive, conceive, and birth a son "I will surely return to you about this time next year, and Sarah your wife will have a son" (Gen. 18:10). Likewise, Manoah's wife was reminded, "You will become pregnant and have a son" and gave her details of how to care for him (Judg.13:5). Mary Magdalene was reminded of her importance as a disciple of Christ as she stood outside the tomb of Jesus crying when He appeared to her and commissioned her with the first gospel of his resurrection, "Jesus said, "Do not hold on to me, for I have not yet ascended to the Father. Go instead to my brothers and tell them, 'I am ascending to my Father and your Father, to my God and your God" (John 20:13-18). And Gideon was reminded that "The Lord is with you, mighty warrior" (Judg. 6:11). Gideon was a mighty warrior! And there are many other examples of God reminding people of their purpose and relationship with Him. What is God reminding you of?

Choosing God and His ways makes you and I a chosen people (1 Pet 2:9). And as a believer, we are in the priesthood of God and therefore have direct access and connection to God, hence silence and stillness. The lineage is passed directly to you, the believer, as your identification from the Lord who gave Himself for you and I, that He might redeem us from all sin and purify unto Himself a peculiar people, zealous of good works (Titus 2:14). God's ID provides you with a description, label, and classification today in this existing structure of society. Your ID carries no threat or potential of being suppressed or constrained, but instead releases the weight of the world off your shoulders to walk, talk, and respond according to who God says you are. You have exactly what you need to victorious. You were born with purpose destined for greatness and deemed God's woman. The whole world and universe were created with you in mind. And if you understand this, then your concerns are on the concerns of God, not merely on human concerns. Human concerns often hinder God's plans for your life. Remember, you are instructed to not worry about such things but seek first the Kingdom of God and His righteousness, and all these things will be given to you as well (Matt 6:25-34).

Don't allow confusion to rule your thoughts, feelings, and actions

~~⌒⌒⌒

-recap of progress-

Let's take a moment now to go over the progress we've made over time. This serves as a reminder of where God has brought us from. As well as, where He's taking us. First, it's worth repeating that identification (ID) created in the beginning secured our place in the world bringing unity to the human race and guaranteeing woman's dignity and worth.

> Genesis 2:21 says, "And the LORD God caused a deep sleep to fall upon Adam, and he slept: and he took one of his ribs, and closed up the flesh instead thereof; v. 22 And the rib, which the LORD God had taken from man, made he a woman, and brought her unto the man."

In an earlier chapter you read where I questioned why God caused Adam to sleep during the time of woman's creation. Because God didn't have to do that, but I was led to understand that "deep sleep" was used for the revelation or uncovering of what was not previ- *uncovering* ously known to man. The prophetic vision of woman was revealed to man after her creation, which meant man was not conscious or involved during this time. God manifested or revealed Himself to woman and man in His own way individually and separate from one another. This has nothing to do with inferiority but rather everything to do with communion, fellowship, and revelation on a personal level. God desires to continue to have this same one-on-one personal relationship with you. Your spiritual connection is just as unique as your soul (thoughts, creativity, etc.) and body.

Reflection Moment: Beauty is connected to woman, but the word beauty has become blurred by the world. Don't carry around the weight of trying to be everything the world wants you to be. True beauty resides in the heart. List inner qualities that truly describe the beauty connected to you.

We are coming out of the traditions where women were known for being responsible of managing the household in the role of wife and mother. Out of the roles of being subordinate to our husband and away from being viewed lower in position. Away from the tradition of the husband being the patriarch of his family (clan) while the wife became part of his family. And away from the man exercising spiritual leadership by presenting the sacrifices and offerings for the family, while women offered a sacrifice after the birth of a child. Religiously, women participated in worship, but it wasn't required because men were only to appear before the Lord. Women had an essential part in the community and were protected within it, but they were often ignored, mistreated, abused, and neglected. Note: godly women were admired, and their contributions were valued. Widows were protected. It's good to know where you came from to see the progress however, today you must not ignore the opportunity and gentle tug inside of you to expand yourself and reach the full potential that you were created for.

ID is key to a successful path

The New Testament offered woman a renewed role
renewed
through God's redemptive plan. Not only is woman
mentioned in the genealogy of Christ, but she (Mary) would be the one to birth the Messiah. She (Mary Magdalene) also followed Jesus, with the multitudes, being included into the parables and illustrations. Yes, Jesus elevated woman (us) back to her proper place. A place with safeguards for rights in marriage, divorce, ministry, and overall life. Jesus spent a great deal of time teaching women, which speaks to your

intelligence and ability to hold an in-depth conversation with great perception and understanding. You identify with The Creator on every level with intense spiritual sensitivity. You are a unique masterpiece. In Ephesians 2:10 we are told, "For we are God's handiwork, created in Christ Jesus to do good works, which God prepared in advance for us to do." And I Corinthians 6:20, "You were bought at a price. Therefore, honor God with your bodies." And if you've forgotten, you are loved as described in I John 4:9-10, "This is how God showed His love among us: He sent His one and only Son into the world that we might live through Him. He sent His Son as an atoning sacrifice for our sins." And finally, you are treasured found in Exodus 19:5, "Now if you obey me fully and keep my covenant, then out of all nations you will be my treasured possession."

You're the only creation "built" with raw resources derived from man. The word built describes your construction *built* being of both previous and existing parts. Existing describes having actual being or life. And isn't that what we embody, life? Life is embedded in the first name woman (Eve) held and the essence of what we're able to produce. Our journey is formed by putting together the law of the Old Testament and restoration to life in the New Testament. God's purpose is evident.

You are designed to receive, hold, sustain, and bring forth life all while being sturdy, sound, and strong. You're the nurturing and supportive element in mankind, creation, and The Kingdom of God. You were never meant to be isolated but rather up-front working alongside of man contributing to the world. Yes, you are designed to go on, even after interruption, built to endure while in constant communion with

God reaching full purpose and success. Note: with God there isn't a possible, hidden, or likely purpose for you because you definitely have purpose. And it's not a matter of being capable of or becoming capable because you're created with the power and ability to fulfill all that God has designed you to be.

~⁀

-all in the name-

A name is a form of ID expressing the essence, character, and nature of a person. The name of *divine truth* God reveals the divine truth of who He is and reveals His character. God's name holds power and holiness under which you are victorious having the authority to speak truth. You are also able to understand the personal revelation and relationship God desires to have with you if only from His name alone. God desires you know Him as:

- El-Berith - God of the Covenant
- El-Elyon - The Most High God/The Exalted One
- El-Olam - God of Eternity/God the Everlasting One
- El-Roi - God who Sees me/God of Vision
- El-Shaddai - God of the Mountains/The Almighty God
- Elohim - plural form for deity. "Let us make man in our image"

Jehovah (YHWH)

- Yahweh-Jireh - The Lord will Provide
- Yahweh-Mekaddesh - The Lord Sanctifies
- Yahweh-Nissi - The Lord is my Banner
- Yahweh-Rohi - The Lord is my Shepherd
- Yahweh-Sabaoth - The Lord of Hosts/The Lord Almighty
- Yahweh-Shalom - The Lord is Peace
- Yahweh-Shammah - The Lord is There
- Yahweh-Tsidkenu - The Lord is Our Righteousness

God desires to be your refuge; safe place. He desires to be your defender and fortress, source of light, and life. God is your purifier; refiner. And although God is beyond your ability to completely understand, He still desires that you know Him. God understands your needs and He will respond. Therefore, as a nurturer, understand your need to lean on the Great Nurturer for renewed strength and wisdom. No one else can do it. God is the giver and sustainer of true life. Life you desire and need.

Reflection Moment: The Aramaic word "Abba" translated means Daddy which is the relationship God wants to have with you (Matt. 6:9). What things do you need to talk to Daddy about?

RECEIVING EQUIPS YOU TO LIVE A SUCCESSFUL LIFE AND SERVE GOD IN ALL CIRCUMSTANCES AND EXPERIENCES.

— BAIN JOHNSON

You set the tone for your purpose, design, and character by being true to who you really are. You are life. And life in itself has movement, grows, and reproduces according to its own kind. And in all movement, there is change in position which comes through the situations and experiences you encounter. Change doesn't have to bad. Learning to flow with progress, development, and embracing change can be a positive experience. Spiritual growth develops confidence in who and who's you are. And then be assured that God's purpose and place for you in His plan are sealed and solid. God loves you. Therefore, obey God refraining from sin. Finally, do not entertain the lies of the enemy of God and remember daily who God is and His promises.

-elevation-

Remember, in the New Testament women reemerge and restrictions are lifted. In Matthew 28:5-10, a woman was chosen to be first to bear witness to Christ's resurrection. She informed the disciples that Jesus (life) had risen from the grave and her words were carried to others also giving life to the hearers re-sparking their zeal, belief, and hope in the risen Savior. This perfect example shows woman's design as a life giver in the spirit (words, worship, and actions). And throughout the New Testament, you continue to see Jesus bringing woman back into ministry, business, and leadership. He confirmed our place in the kingdom and our role within creation and mankind.

Understand any encounter with The Savior involves worship. Worship is your human acknowledgment, humility, and response to the self-revelation of who God is. As you draw closer, you come to know Him as Father and The Source of all that's needed. Psalm 103:13 says, "As a father has compassion on his children, so the Lord has compassion on those who fear Him". He is a Father of mercies (2 Cor. 1:3).

Mary of Magdala worshipped with a box of expensive oil and tears. Tears filled with life's experiences poured from her soul. This tells you that there's something miraculous that happens when sincere humility, conscious of your unworthiness, meets His grace, compassion, and love. This kind of offering is a sacrifice which leads you into intense worship where God meets and hears you. Mary of Magdala, who poured out all she had at the feet of Jesus, was chosen to prepare Him for His burial. What an honor! Note: anytime you pour your soul out before The Savior, you will also receive. Receive? Yes, peace, renewed life, balance, joy, forgiveness, grace, and mercy that surpasses all under-standing. May our response be like Mary of Magdala to the awareness of the holy presence of God. It's within the space of worship where God reveals Himself personally. Today, God is seeking true worshippers who can worship in spirit and truth. This is your calling.

ID reveals the plan of God

Many women were active in the Bible. To highlight a few, you can look at:

- Esther is a heroine who was a Jewish orphan who became queen not revealing she was a Jew until a plot/decree was made to all who would not bow down would be killed. God used her to revoke the decree to destroy the Jews.
- Lydia is known as the first European converted to Christ under the preaching of Paul. Her wealth allowed her to live independently. She hosted Paul and his entourage in Philippi after her conversion.
- Deborah is known for her role in leading Israel during the time of the judges. In a patriarchal society, it was extremely noteworthy that God used her to lead Israel out of danger.

> Other valued contributors were Hannah, Abigail
> Naomi, Ruth.

Finally, you carry life in a wider sense than mankind. As a woman, you take and support life from one phase to another. Pregnancy is one example of supporting life physically. Spiritually, you support life by transporting life in your thinking, understanding, emotions, attitudes, and intentions. Again, God is the giver of life, and life is a gift that you receive, bear, give, lift up, and transfer. Your design is capable of containing life, holding life, bearing the weight of life, and taking a leading part in life. Your design carries the original signature and awe of God's complete goodness. God will never abandon you.

Reflection Moment: God takes your experiences and reshapes them into valuable purpose. Recall an experience where you know it was turned around and reshaped for your good.

-*love*-

Love is a profound combination of emotions and feelings that bring about strong affections and an attachment. While love can be a positive emotion and feeling, unfortunately for many women love has mounted up to emotional disappointments. Disappointments that cause the heart (soul) to become callous blocking out people and even blocking out God. Note: bad relationships can emotionally damage you stealing your joy and suppressed emotions from abuse, unfaithfulness, insensitivity (type of neglect), ect. can turn into deep rooted hurt bringing brokenness, depression, or a state of existing.

Spiritual love is a relationship of self-giving as a result of God's action in Christ. In the Bible, Paul described love (Greek word agape) as the more excellent way than tongues or even preaching (I Cor. 13:1). The other love, on a physical level (Greek word eros), is a natural emotion (Greek word phileo) that moves and reacts, bypassing the spirit. Your first desire should be the love (agape) described as coming from the spirit and aligned with the order of your triune being. This love is not simply an emotion. This love is faithful and does not fade away.

> Three Greek words that translate into the English word love:
>
> Agape refers to the self-sacrificing love of God for humanity which was reciprocated and practiced towards God and among one another.
>
> Philia is defined as an affection that is either brotherhood or generally non-sexual affection
>
> Eros is defined as an affection of a sexual nature

Understanding the greatest commandment to love the Lord thy God with all thy heart, soul, and mind (Matt. 22:37) is knowing that this commandment is the basis of all other commandments. This love is not to be based off of emotions but rather a dis- *disciplined will* ciplined will. Without a disciplined will, love is likely to be misused and applied to areas where spiritual love should be. Note: on the surface physical love may look and feel great to the body but it will keep you held emotionally hostage based off a brief emotion. Now, this commandment to love is then followed-up with, love your neighbor as yourself. In order to love your neighbor, you must first love yourself. This makes a lot of sense because how can you begin to love someone else properly if you've not first learned to love you? "To love you" basically means that you love who God made you to be. And this is something that satan doesn't want you to do. Thus, in order begin to love you, you cannot base it off the world's often misguided perception of women nor can you absorb degrading experiences you may have suffered that tried to define you. Instead, you must embrace the mirror reflection you see physically and most importantly, the inner reflection that truly exuberates the beautiful you that you are.

Jesus directs you to the fact that He has loved you. Love is an action. John 3:16 says, "For God so loved the world that he gave his one and only Son, that whoever believes in him shall not perish but have eternal life." Love is self-giving (Gal. 5:13-15) and you should be characterized by your walk-in love. If you walk in the Spirit, you will not fulfil the lust of your body (Gal. 5:16). By this, you can offer your bodies as a living sacrifice holy and pleasing to God—this is your true and proper worship (Rom. 12:1). And then, Paul said, "The law is fulfilled in love." Jesus fulfilled the law by His love. Your proper response to God's grace should be unreserved love and obedience. Mankind's love will fail you at some point, but a relationship with God never fails. It will sustain you in times of human failed love. God will never forget nor forsake you.

> A disciplined will involves self-control, self-restraint, practice, preparation, governance (commandments), and will.

Love is a response that increases
your holiness before God

Gifts work in you, filling you (Gal. 5:22,23) and are evident in your service towards others as a witness of God (Acts 1:8). God's gifts, like His plans, are not limited to any race or gender but are designed for all. Therefore, receive, exercise, and pour out your gifts back into humanity as a service towards others. By doing this, internal voids will be filled as yet another example of "pouring yet receiving" mysteries of God's inner workings! What causes voids? Living outside of the will and intent of God for life. Perhaps this explains how and why even someone with everything, the world says will make you happy, is often the one plummeting to destruction through the vices of this world.

Every gift is a gift with purpose! Living inside the will of God ensures fulfilling purpose which reaches beyond self and into humanity. Love is the greatest gift of the spirit. You will know and demonstrate that the Spirit is at work in your life and the life of others when the following is displayed:

Joy - happiness resulting from a right relation with God; not obtained by your own efforts. Joy is experienced in good times as well as bad times (1 Peter 1:6). Peace surpasses all understanding, will guard your hearts & minds (Phil. 4:7)

Longsuffering – patience that increases, with others, the more we become like Christ (2 Peter 3:9)

Kindness – helpful and good towards others with a tender heart, forgiving one another, just as God in Christ also forgave you (Eph. 4:32)

Faithfulness – dependable like God compassionate without fail (Lam. 3:22,23)

Worship - an attitude of worship toward God in spiritual songs,
singing and thankfulness in your heart to the Lord for
all things (Eph. 5:19,20)

Gentleness – soft touch, calm reassurance, and loving hand. This is
illustrated to a shepherd caring for his flock of lambs
(Isa. 40:11). God spoke in a gentle whisper to Elijah
(1 Kings 19:11-13)

Self-Control - a sober, temperate, calm, and dispassionate
approach to life. Capable of mastering personal
desires and passions. A self-disciplined life following Christ's example of being in the world but
not of the world.

*Art is determined by value and how much
someone will pay for it at any given moment
Know Jesus paid the ultimate price for you*

God provides you with true meaning and significance in scripture.
Key qualities, essential nature, and likeness to God connects you with
nature, mankind, and each other as women. Thus, in your likeness and
connection to God you share the following:

Emotions – give love & receive love. Be angry. Express and feel emotions.

Personality – think and communicate as a rational being. Have a personal identity separating you from other rational beings and non-living things. Communicate to others.

Creativity – create meaningful new ideas. As God created the universe and everything within it. You also can be creative transcending traditional ideas, rules, patterns, etc. creating meaningful new ideas.

Morality – sense right and wrong. Know and understand the difference between good and evil. However, God does not have the capacity to choose evil; humanity does.

Hope and faith are connected to love

Reflection Moment: Eve, means life. To live is to carry, enjoy, maintain, own, seize, and be involved with life. Are you living a purposed life?

-truth-

God is truth. Truth is reliable and can be trusted. So, in a world that constantly tries to throw a false reflection of who you are, it's your job is to know the truth. It's your job to know God. And do not swerve from truth. Truth is not simply a matter of suggesting accuracy; truth is accuracy (Rom. 2:8; Gal. 5:7). For God's work is perfect and all His ways are just (Deut. 32:4). He *accuracy* maintains covenant and steadfast love with you as the true and living God. His truth is not only reflected in His commandments but also is reflected in life. It's reflected in His faithfulness and justice, and it's reflected in Jesus prayer (John 17:17-19) to "Sanctify them by the truth; your word is truth. As you sent me into the world, I have sent them into the world. For them I sanctify myself, that they too may be truly sanctified." You, as a follower of Christ, are of the truth and everyone who is for the truth hears His voice (John 18:37). Receiving Jesus is followed by walking in truth or in the light (2 John 1:4). And everyone who does evil hates the Light and doesn't want to come into the Light because they fear their deeds will be exposed. That's worth rereading! But you who practice the truth come into the Light so it may be seen clearly what we do is accomplished in God (John 3:20-21). Therefore, you cannot say you have a relationship with God and still walk in darkness. This is not practicing the truth.

And you, belonging to the truth, listens to the voice of God. Why? Because He is "the way, the truth, and the life" (John 14:6). Jesus left the Holy Spirit (Helper, Comforter) with you after his ascension who directs you towards truth. In John 15:26-27, it tells us that when the Holy Spirit comes that it is the Spirit of truth who proceeds from the Father testifying about Jesus, and it's our job to also testify because we were with Him from the beginning. Jeremiah 1:5 says, that before He formed you in the womb, He knew you. Before you were born He set you apart appointing you as a prophet to the nations. God, who set you apart from your mother's womb, and called you by His grace, was pleased (Gal. 1:15). "My frame was not hidden from you when I was made in the secret place, when I was woven together in the depths of the earth (Ps. 139:15). Again, the truth that God ordained you even before you were born is so amazing! This really tells you that your life has purpose.

While addressing truth, it's important to know that you will not find satisfaction in the things of this world. In the end, it's only what you do for Christ that will last. And its only God who can satisfy the profound thirst of your soul for life's meaning and significance. Let that sink in. Matthew chapter 6 says it best, "But store up for yourselves treasures in heaven, where moths and vermin do not destroy, and where thieves do not break in and steal. For where your treasure is, there your heart will be also." This should make you look at things differently. Because here the world and its success are viewed in an entirely different way with new insight. Make it a point to practice seeing things with spiritual eyes. Receive life from the Living God and demonstrate gratitude to God for this great gift of life. It's this attitude that yields wisdom. Wisdom that comes from heaven is first of all pure, then full of peace-loving, considerate, submissive, full of mercy and good fruit that is impartial and sincere (James 3:17).

-*gratitude*-

It's a sincere inward appreciation for the things that God provides each day, and it begins when you *appreciation* see the wonderful grace of God taking in all of God's provisions down to the smallest details with thankfulness. This choice is choosing to look for good, not evil, which includes the good in people. Gratitude is trusting that all things are working together for the good, refusing to think evil, and rejoicing in the truth. This is even when truth can only be found in the hope of a future as good. Now, it's interesting there is a connection between the word "blessed" and the Hebrew word "knee" signifying an association and reaction of kneeling before God for His blessings. Blessings which are the result of humbling yourselves before God. Also, gratitude expresses thanks for the gift of life even when you're having a bad day. Yes, there is always something to be grateful for even if it's remembering that you woke up with the breath of God. Remember to look at the details all around you that you may take for granted. Remind yourself that things could always be worse and focus on what's left. This eliminates bitterness, anger, resentment, envy, and lack of sympathy towards others and their struggles.

Find the beauty in God, people, circumstances, and life.

You will have tribulations, but Jesus assures you in John 14:27 that, "Peace I leave with you; my peace I give you. I do not give to you as the world gives. Do not let your hearts be troubled and do not be afraid." God will preserve the soul of the one who looks to Him for help. Yes, He will both preserve the soul and keep you from evil guarding your life. He will guard your coming and going forever (Ps. 121). Hide this in your heart when trials come. And guard your heart remaining connected to the Lord because everything you do flows from the heart (Prov. 4: 23). In Matthew 12:35 it says, "the good person brings good things out of the good stored up in him, and an evil person brings evil things out of the evil stored up in him." Let that sink in. Love given away is always backed up by heaven. Whoever sows sparingly will reap sparingly but whoever sows bountifully will also reap bountifully (2 Cor. 9:6).

It's all about perspective and attitude. If your focus is on what's wrong you'll most likely start blaming others for your misery. Others like Eve for being deceived, disobeying God, and eating from the forbidden tree. I mean of all the trees Eve! Really!? But you face the same choices to obey or disobey God today. How have you done with that? You can choose life or you can choose to rebel. The choice is yours to make but be advised, choosing flesh leads to darkness and destruction where there will be no one to blame but yourself. The Lord promises that this world and its elements will pass away with fervent heat, but you (the believer) will be established before Him forever in the new heavens and earth (2 Peter 3:10-13; Rev. 21:1). Yes, the world will pass away and the lusts within, but those who do the will of God shall abide forever (1 John 2:17). Keep love ever before your mind and heart and you will remain in God. God is good and desires good for you.

-seven-

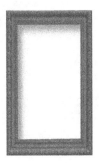

the journey

journey

| jour•ney |

Passage or progress from one stage to another

course suitable for progress

course of life

G aining traction along the journey requires that you practice meditation and repentance due to The Law of the Lord being within your mind and inscribed upon your heart (Jer. 31:33) while aiming towards walking out the commandments and listening for the Holy Spirit. God sees and knows exactly where you are on the journey. In Proverbs 15:3 we are told, "The eyes of the Lord are in every place, beholding the evil and the good." His eyes are throughout the earth strengthening the righteous (2 Chron. 16:9). Do not think for one moment that God does not see or understand your struggles, anxieties, fears, etc. Neither is He too far to reach you. God is your refuge and strength, an ever-present help in trouble. Therefore, do not bargain with the world exchanging eternal peace for temporary comfort. Do not be lured off course by the vices of the enemy. Instead, trust in God which yields true inner peace. Proverbs 29:25 says, "The fear of man bringeth a snare: but whoso putteth his trust in the Lord shall be safe."

Be fully conscious of and thankful for the revelations being written upon your hearts

Being honest, I'm sure my hand was raised for the easy life filled with happiness, victory, and success. However, reality quickly illuminated that both victory and adversity were going to be on this journey. Although the latter is often ignored and *adversity* avoided, it's the one that somehow catches you off guard every time it happens. However, it shouldn't because adversity is often the tool that keeps you close to God. Nobody wants to hear that, but if you learn to look at adversity differently, it helps the journey toward progress and purpose go a lot smoother. In Jeremiah 29:11, the Word reminds you that God's thoughts toward you are of peace and not evil to give you an expected end. So why does adversity exist? First, remember the original order of the world which was designed and deemed good by God (Gen. 1:31). Suffering and hardships didn't exist until both woman and man sinned, disobeying God, which brought suffering, adversity, pain, disease, death, difficult circumstances, hardships, etc. into the world. These were consequences of their choices. Consequences that not only affected you and I but all creation. For creation groans to be freed (Rom. 8:18-22).

Adversity is permitted so that we learn to stop sinning and turn to God who offers grace, mercy, and forgiveness through His son (Isa. 53:5-6). Yes, the road will have straightaways, but it will have bumps too, which doesn't mean that God is not there, it means that the world is still broken. Therefore, try to aim your focus on the world God created; not the world man desecrated. This isn't turning a blind eye to poverty, exploitation, hunger, etc. but through the lens of God, you can embrace the journey and purpose you are called to with clarity realizing God never desired sin/bad things for the world. But because sin crept in we are told... God so loved the world, being you and I, that He gave His only son and whosoever believeth in him should not perish but have everlasting life (John 3:16).

> The world was designed to be good but was infiltrated with evil. God allowed man and woman to make a choice (free will) to obey/disobey His Word. And God also allowed consequences of sin.

-adversity-

Adversity doesn't stop the plans of God. In the Bible Mary, the mother of Jesus, faced adversity with rejection by her community. Esther risked her life to save the Jewish people from destruction. Ruth was widowed early in life and Naomi embraced Ruth the Moabite within the family of Judah. And there are many more women in whom God fulfilled His purpose in their lives even though adversity was present. Again, adversity doesn't stop the plans of God, you just have to learn to live (silence and stillness) through it. In the midst of both adversity and disappointments God is there, He's listening, He hears your cries, and He will rescue you. God has plans for your disappointments regardless of the situation, and He works through them all to prosper you and give you hope. Thus, choose not to be bitter and hold unforgiveness in your heart. Instead open your fist and raise your hands to the will of God even when you don't understand why things happen. Personally, I know facing the journey with God is a lot easier than without Him. Keep on moving forward knowing that God will vindicate you and defend you, just wait patiently and confidently for the Lord (Ps. 37:6-8). Release

anything and that takes momentum away from your progress towards
purpose.   *release*

> Moving forward requires that you heal from past offenses
> and stop living out of wounded places. You have to let go
> of who hurt you, how you were raised, and offenses that
> keep you in a space of replaying it over and over in your
> head. How you deal with adversity determines your pace on
> the journey. This doesn't excuse the behavior or the pain
> it caused but it offers forgiveness so you can go on and ful-
> fill purpose.

There will be times when all you can do is cry out to God for help.
Help for the struggles, heartache, troubles, and pain. There may not
even be words to adequately express what you're feeling, but in these
moments turn to God. I like Psalm 71 where it says so well, "In thee,
O Lord, do I put my trust: let me never be put to confusion. Deliver
me in thy righteousness, and cause me to escape: incline thine ear unto
me, and save me. Be thou my strong habitation, whereunto I may continually resort: thou hast given commandment to save me; for thou art
my rock and my fortress." The journey utilizes every circumstance and
experience to prepare you for the world and your role within it. It often
brings about compassion that you would otherwise not have known,
making you grateful and humble. You may not have raised your hand
for adversity, like me, but take this life God has blessed you with and
choose the path forward. The Lord knows the way of the righteous (Ps.
1:6). Trust in His provision for justification and acceptance through

the sacrifice of Jesus as your ransom for sin. Jesus, The Son of God; equal to God, humbled himself taking on the form of a servant made in the likeness of man and offered Himself up. "Therefore God exalted him to the highest place and gave him the name that is above every name, that at the name of Jesus every knee should bow, in heaven and on earth and under the earth, and every tongue acknowledge that Jesus Christ is Lord, to the glory of God the Father" (Phil. 2:9-11). It's clear that it's your confession of God's Son as Lord that brings understanding to the journey because without it you are literally lost. There is no other name by which you can be saved (Acts 4:12).

To fully walk in and enjoy the journey, you need to release the past; not allowing it to consume your mind. I know that is being repeated but very necessary to understand. Then rest in knowing that everything you've been through will be effective and affective in the world. Walking in the spirit brings focus to what God has placed inside of you and how that can be of service to others. You can focus on opportunities to be a light in this dark world while being aware of those things that will try to pull you back into sin, past offenses, hurts, etc. Note: this is accomplished by remaining in stillness which ensures spiritual awareness. Be assured, the journey is more than birth and death. It includes everything in-between too. Within "the dash" separating birth and death, two great life points, is your journey. The journey advances and stretches you into purpose. Now, it's important to remember that while moving forward you will also encounter change. Change is something different from what you know, and it's the transformation needed to make you fit for the journey. Transformation makes you capable, competent, prepared, and qualified for everything that will occur in life. And without change, you remain in a condition of not moving, stagnant, ceasing to live, and failing to develop. This does not coincide with the journey. If you've ever felt like you were born to do more, that's God's gentle tug on your heart that there is more to life than what you're doing. And in order to do more you need to embrace, seek, and accept change. To be clear, change can cause a disruption in your normal, but this disruption produces the results needed for progress along the course of life. The Bible mentions change as a life that no longer conforms to the ways of the world but to one that pleases God (Rom. 12:2). Change renews your mind which will manifest itself through your actions and bearing of fruit in every good work and growing in the knowledge of God (Col. 1:10). Similar to adversity, change draws us near to God through the blood of Christ (Eph. 2:13).

You will make mistakes but being loyal to a mistake is resisting the call of God to change. Having the courage to correct a mistake shows you're growth in your walk with God. Only be faithful in obedience to God who will strengthen you. Don't let a wrong judgement obstruct progress. Instead, receive God's truth, His promises, and His correction. This is understanding the call placed on your life as God continues to lead you on the journey. In the book of Isaiah 14:27 it says, nothing can stop His plan for your life. No one can delete, eliminate, or wipe out the plans God has for you. Obey the commandments of The Lord and follow them (Deut. 28:13) realizing you're more than a conqueror (Rom. 8:37). You can do all things through Christ Jesus who gives you strength (Phil. 4:13). God opens your eyes to true purpose which gives life. You are truly made for His glory (Isa. 43:7). It's only when you don't seek and obey God that you miss the beauty of life's purpose.

> Purpose draws you to the cross of Jesus (John 6:44). Therefore, let the desires of your heart be centered on God as you seek Him with your whole heart.

God is in the midst of the world and in the midst of you

The journey is a process of refinement that shapes and forms you to become as pure as gold. This process frees you from impurities and anything that does not please God. We try to look good on the outside but refinement elevates inner qualities that look good to God. Now, we've all acted in ways that deaden our sense of spirituality simply for our own selfish pleasure. We've been stubborn in denial of our shortcomings and possibly have lacked compassion for others. Refinement has a way of reducing you to a purer state for moral cleansing. Psalm 51:7 says that you can then come to God in prayer knowing He wants a broken spirit and a contrite heart. In other words, to be humble and repentant before God which is being crushed by the sense of guilt and sinfulness. God will revive the spirit of such a one (Isa. 57:15) and this one will be exalted. Indeed the journey is a test of faith. Faith being the assurance of what we hope for and the certainty of what we do not see (Heb. 11:1). And ironically, faith shines best in the midst

faith

of adversity. For without faith it is impossible to please God (Heb. 11:6).

Perform self-checks to ensure you are submitted under the authority of God who sheds light on obstacles and distractions aimed to hinder the journey. Note: the enemy is against God and His purposes which includes His purpose for you. Always respond to noises and distractions to confirm that you know the truth about who you are and who is leading you. Your response speaks to the atmosphere with authority over the enemy (Luke 10:19). No response, is a response that says you're unsure.

Release fear. Fear will only hinder your walk affecting you spiritually, mentally, and physically. God has not given you the spirit of fear but of power, love, and a sound mind (2 Tim. 1:7). Having power is the ability to act and produce an effect. An effect like love. Love is unselfish, loyal, and benevolent concern for another's well-being, and sound mind is a disciplined self-controlled mind. That's worth reading again. Fear, on the other hand, causes you to overreact to situations that trigger experiences of hurt, frustration, or trauma placing you back on the scene of yesterday and not today moving forward. By nurturing fear, it causes you to question God's Word and authority which is something you definitely do not want to do. This is the trick of the enemy which was played in beginning with Eve and Adam. Fear can be defeated with the Word of God. Finally, you're equipped for the journey because whatever God starts He also completes. Just keep moving forward. Remember, feelings are not always reality. And fear comes to steal, kill, and destroy but God gives abundant life (John 10:10).

Reflection Moment: Charm is deceptive and beauty does not last but a woman who fears the Lord will be greatly praised (Exod. 14:14). What does this scripture mean to you?

-rest-

God rested on the seventh day after ending His work of creation. From His example, we should not overlook rest along the journey. Rest not only refreshes but provides you with an interval in life to repose yourself in order to go on. Within rest you find relief and freedom from troubles that clog the mind. It's also a support device, when under affliction, sustaining you. It's important to find rest in God so that you can further support mankind. Matthew 11:28-30 tells us to, "Come to me, all you who are weary and burdened, and I will give you rest. Take my yoke upon you and learn from me, for I am gentle and humble in heart, and you will find rest for your souls. For my yoke is easy and my burden is light." Without it there is a guaranteed exhaustion, distress, frustration, and pain that drains you spiritually, mentally, and physically. This journey requires calmness, peacefulness, and serenity let your thoughts be on things that are true, honest, just, pure, lovely, of good report, things of virtue, and praiseworthy (Phil.4:8).

Resting ultimately returns you spiritually to proper alignment. A space deemed good and accessible with the confession of your sins to God who cleanses you from all unrighteousness (1 John 1:9). Now within rest, silence can also be found as you connect spirit to Spirit. In addition, rest is found by recalling the Word of God and His promises in moments of unrest putting you back into the place where you can hear God and receive further directions for the journey. *promises* God promises to supply every need you have (Phil. 4:19), that His grace is sufficient for you (2 Cor. 12:9), that His children will not be overtaken with temptation (1 Cor. 10:13), you have victory over death (Acts 2:32, 1 Cor. 15), all things work together for good to those who love and serve Him (Rom. 8:28), those who believe in Jesus and are baptized for the forgiveness of sins will be saved (Mark 16:16), you, as a believer, will have eternal life (John 10:27,28). That's something you can rest in.

> God will never leave you nor forsake you (Heb. 13:5). You are His masterpiece fearfully and wonderfully made (Ps. 139:13–14). The Spirit of God made you and gives you life (Job 33:4). You are created in Christ Jesus for good works consecrated appointed as a prophet to the nations (Jer. 1:5). You were prepared beforehand for good works (Eph. 2:10) for you did not choose God, God choose you that you should live and bear fruit, so whatever you ask the Father in Jesus name, He will give it to you (John 15:16). Amen.

God gives life

You're equipped for the journey which means you have the ability to progress despite life's hurdles. With a made-up mind, you can push through physical and emotional obstacles to victory. Now, victory may look different from what you thought it would but have no doubt success over the enemy is yours. Rest assured, God is with you and fighting for you. Be strong and courageous without fear (Deut. 31:6). Seek to have characteristics that produce endurance, perseverance, and unmovable faith for the next step in the course of life. These qualities will be important to have, especially at intersections where choices demand your response. Finally, let God be The Good Shephard that He is leading and guiding you. The steps of a good man/woman are ordered by the Lord (Ps. 37:23). Be doers of the Word and not hearers only (James 1:22). Maintain a "yes" lifestyle before the Holy Spirit being obedient to the Word of God. Let your "yes" not only change you but the lives of others and opens doors you would not believe (John 16:33). Say yes to God's will for your life.

- forward-

The path is not always a straight line. There are bumps and turns but the results don't change. Proverbs 3:5-6 tells you to trust in the Lord with all your heart, lean not on your own understanding but in all of your ways acknowledge Him, and then He will direct your path. The tools you pick up along the way are: knowing the voice of God, learning to trust and believe in God's Word, and going on even when you don't understand everything. The answer may not be what you want it to be all the time, but know that God is Sovereign and He is directing your path. You just have to keep going forward. This brings us to, endurance and perseverance. These are tools that sharpen determination and strengthen the faith muscle. Maintaining a steady pace on this journey, through stillness, is important because the race is not given to the swift, nor the strong, but to the one who endures to the end (Eccles. 9:11). Keeping a steady pace is still movement, growth, and progress.   *pace*

As you continue onward, know that God will not tell you anything contrary to His Word. This is where knowing the voice of God, commandments of God, and Word of God is key. In John 10:27 it says, the sheep know the voice of The Shepherd. Now, there will come a time, or two, or three when you will have to release things that slow you down and don't serve you anymore on the journey. It may be hard to do but not impossible. And oftentimes, it may be a test of your faith which has to do with the condition of you heart. So, even when things don't make sense, lean not on your own understanding, trust that God knows what He's doing. And don't talk yourself out of elevating into the completed WOA you're becoming. For the promises of God are yes and amen (2 Cor. 1:20). Forget the things that are behind and stretch to that which is ahead (Phil. 3:13). Note: examine feelings and emotions against the truth of God's Word, weeding out the lies.

Let your gifts and talents lead you towards God; not away. Every gift is intended to glorify Him. Those who neglect God, neglect some portion of their being (spirit, soul, and body). Therefore, stir up the gifts that are within.

The Spirit brings perspective

Trust the process. It's not always about what you lost but rather what is left. God always uses what's left in your hand for His glory. Every experience makes you stronger and wiser for the journey ahead. Again, no one raises their hand for adversity but it will come and when it does may your faith light the way to victory. This again brings us to the tool God uses which is obedience. God calls you to obedience especially in the midst of adversity. In Deuteronomy 31:6 it says, "Be strong and courageous. Do not be afraid or terrified because of them, for the LORD your God goes with you; he will never leave you or forsake you". Yes, God will go before you and be with you, He promises to never leave you nor forsake you. In Numbers 23:19, it tells you that God is not like man/woman, He can be trusted; doesn't lie. Knowing this should make the journey more enjoyable. Therefore, take time to soak in the beauty of life around you, knowing that God will accomplish His will in your life. You will finish your course. Again, simply trust the process, anticipate, and look for God. Don't compare your journey with someone else's journey because we're all different and God works with us individually.

-*battle & reveal*-

By now, you should know there is a constant battle occurring for your soul right now. God is pulling you toward Him and His purposes while the enemy (satan) is pulling you toward enticements and tricks in hopes of derailing and causing you to disobey to God. With that being said, God always provides a way of escape for His children, *escape* it's you who must choose to accept the way He provides.

You are made to endure. So, regardless of what picture the world portrays of woman, God tells you the truth about who you are. In Galatians 5:7 it says, "You were running a good race. Who cut in on you to keep you from obeying the truth?" During these times keep your focus on the course and make it your priority to remain connected and aligned to God. Sometimes focusing on the course involves looking ahead to where you're going knowing the experience at hand is not the end all. Continuously meditate on His Word acting upon all that is written in it to remain centered. Note: while it's good, within context, to have human acceptance it should never supersede God's acceptance. Human acceptance will never be satisfied.

Truth is not just accuracy but it's something that should be obeyed. Truth is opposed to evil. And the truth of God is reflected in His commandments and creation.

Understanding the beginning of woman is essential
to understanding the journey and purpose in this world.

God reveals Himself to you through 1) creation, purpose, rebellion, punishment, restoration; and 2) reestablishment and redemption of woman. You don't have the spirit of the world but rather the Spirit that comes from God in order to receive everything He gives to you freely. Now, as an established and redeemed woman you embody the gift of orderliness in the home and world. Remember, in the *orderliness* beginning woman entered a work already in progress which is not much different than today's woman entering new areas of corporations and other organizations already in progress. You provide effective support to maintain, plan, structure, and organize just to name a few things you bring to the table. Also, in the beginning woman was tasked to keep creation in its existing state; preserving from failure or decline. Yes, I'm confident this task was done with creativity and inspiration because woman had to be secure and confident within herself in order to accomplish this task. In fact, Genesis 2:22 says, God "made He a woman" which can be translated "built He a woman." Being "built" denotes she was established, rebuilt, and made to continue even after interruption; endure. Thus, woman is sturdy and sound, strong, accepted, and recognized.

Woman is essential to the ministry

> BEING LOYAL TO
>
> MISTAKE IS
>
> RESISTING THE
>
> CALL OF GOD TO
>
> CHANGE.
>
> RAIN JOHNSON

You are confident, bold, and empowered. Woman is known for utilizing and managing resources. Our leader- *leadership* ship role, from the beginning, gave us strength preventing weakness or frailty. We're supportive, always there for others, considering other's feelings over our own which bonds and connects us with mankind. Yes, our natural inherent strengths are contributions toward humanity. In the Word of God woman's accounts are acknowledged in creation, establishment, importance, and influence on family and society. The Old Testament, paints woman as being subjected to the will and protection of her husband, honored for performing important roles such as wife and mother. There are moments where we see her rise above those roles leading the Jewish nation in times of crisis. However, the New Testament paints woman anew by Jesus and later Paul who elevated her status again to full participant in the kingdom of God. Women were encouraged to reclaim their place in the body of Christ with a spirit of freedom. Jesus removed the rigid tradition of men and their restrictions showing everyone that religion is a matter of the heart not of the law. Woman was transformed and restored in her identity and purpose. She was involved in the kingdom work and her life experience was illuminated. Jesus positioned women to learn as disciples and recognized her intelligence and commitment. This is seen in interactions and teachings throughout The Bible with woman as main characters. Jesus appealed to woman through housekeeping experiences and elevated her experiences by likening them to God's activity. Her financial support to the work of the kingdom was also received. Woman was viewed as a person and not an object or lesser counterpart to man.

> You are called woman because Eve was taken out of man (Gen 2:23). This name is associated with her relation to Adam; a relation she was created to fulfill. Both man and woman were called "Adam" (Gen 5:2) implying the divine ideal for man and wife is not just by association but a permanent unity; made "one flesh" and given one name. The distinction in Eve is the meaning "life" or "living." For woman is an embodiment of life as we carry and represent life. Life is designed to be owned, enjoyed, retained, kept, and maintained. Life offers restoration and revival. Yes, woman embodies and carries, cares for, protects, and nourishes all life.

Woman's gift of supporting expands toward
the mind and spirit of all those around us

The Word points out that Jesus responded to woman's touch. He healed woman and received her emotional support many *touch* times. Jesus recognized her insight, feelings, spoke theology with her as co-laborers commending her gifts, and faithfulness. Remember, it was a woman who was allowed to anoint Jesus. He recognized her understanding (spiritually sensitivity) of His real mission. And she was commended for her acts of love toward Him. The New Testament dismissed any remaining restrictions placed on woman solely based on sex and race. Barriers were broken and no double standards remained. New possibilities of living were reopened under Jesus' directive, placing woman in early ministry. Again, woman proclaimed the first gospel at the tomb after the resurrection broadcasting Jesus' victory over death. And Christ revealed Himself to woman as the Messiah calling attention to her loyalty in following Christ all the way to the cross and the grave. Her support toward Jesus redefined and reestablished her place within creation.

God reveals inner beauty. He points out the face which reflects His glory as the heavens declare His glory. You also reflect The Creator's splendor, majesty, and manifestation of life. It's the Holy Spirit who drapes your total being with light and beauty just as He adorned the earth and universe. You are considered a friend and disciple of God with intellect and talent(s). You're noted as excellent communicators and detail oriented which was displayed in the proclamation of Jesus' resurrection. Great emphasis was placed on your character and spiritual qualities, not wealth nor physical appearance. You express a marvelous truth within your design. As a Work Of Art you carry His signature and stamp of approval. And you are no doubt beautiful.

*God is life in the absolute sense
and all life depends on Him*

-progress-

As discussed earlier, our role was restored, enlarged, and transformed by Jesus. We were put back into the place *restored* of living out true life. And while the consequences of sin are real, God's grace and mercy are also reflected in the portrait of woman. Everything about woman was received by Jesus and responded to. Now, there is a lot to learn from the woman in Mark 5:32-33 when Jesus asked, "Who touched my garments?" The woman who touched Him "fell down before him, and told him all the truth." Here you may wonder why did God ask a question He knew the answer to? It's by the confession of our mouth that we are saved (Rom. 10:9-13). Her faith and belief in Jesus healed her.

God has not forgotten you, He sees you. Open up your spirit, heart, and mouth and tell Him "all the truth." God will mend the broken places and restore you. For the promises of God are irrevocable. He is a God that cannot lie. So put all trust and confidence in Him. Let your decisions and actions demonstrate your trust in God and let your faith raise the bar of possibilities. We are told in 1 Samuel 12:24, "But be sure to fear the Lord and serve him faithfully with all your heart; consider what great things he has done for you."

God's interactions and teachings were transforming. A few examples are: 1) Mary Magdalene was exercised of seven demons; a spiritual or physical illness. Her encounter was not only one of deliverance but one of inclusion in the inner circle of Jesus; 2) the woman caught in adultery was offered a change of lifestyle. While her actions were not right, Jesus did not subject her to a double standard of her male accusers (John 7:53 – 8:11); 3) the sinful woman who was accepted and received by Jesus to anoint Him. It was her belief and repentance that flowed with her tears (emotions) for The Savior that was heard and made her whole; 4) Mary (mother of Jesus) received the privilege and honor of carrying (supporting) through divine maternity (Luke 1:34-35) The Savior from birth and ultimately to death at the foot of the cross as Jesus gave up the Spirit back to the Father. Mary emphasized a mother's love. Her support and great faith enabled her to be used as an agent of God. Mary's life represented goodness and deep commitment to the ways of God. She witnessed the first public miracle of Jesus changing water to wine, and she was present in the upper room experience in Jerusalem. Finally, Eve, the first woman, was made in the image of God (Gen. 1:26-27) and deemed perfect. In Hebrew, Eve (Chavah/ Havah) meant "living one" or "source of life." Remember that you support the preservation of life on earth. God is your strength, shield, and breath. You are not created to "suck it up" and make it on your own. Run to God. Talk with Him. He will be there to wrap His loving arms around you to guide you on this path of life. Receive daily from God so you can remain effective and complete.

*You are a composition of many beautiful parts
combined to form a whole balanced design*

～

-good news-

You are a composition of many combined beautiful parts forming a whole balanced design. While we share a common bond as women, you are still an individual. It's not a cliché, there really is only one you. You are unique just like your fingerprints, DNA, thoughts, and perception. Now you may have characteristics or traits *unique* similar to your parents, but you are unique and different separated by distinguishing actions. You truly convey a message, like art, that stimulates thoughts, emotions, beliefs, and ideas. Now with that being said, today more women are entering the job market in areas not previously occupied by women. You are critical because you have the ability to see into areas needing improvement with fresh perspective that may have been overlooked. You are created to excel and ordained to be His workmanship.

While sin attempts to separate you from The Father, Jesus put sin away by the sacrifice of Himself (Heb. 9:26). Jesus destroyed the works of satan (1 John 3:8) and covered sin so that it no longer keeps you from being received by the Father. Therefore, in all of your ways believe, accept, and commit to following the way of Jesus, confessing Him as Lord. Remember, faith is the substance of things we hope for, the evidence of things not seen (Heb. 11:1). You are resilient, with the power and ability to return to your original form and position after being bent, compressed, or stretched. You adjust to and recover from adversity and major life changes. Is it easy? No, but it's possible. You entered a world functioning and still added value to its operation. You have a womb that carries and brings forth life. And a body that heals, adjust, and recovers from the miracle of childbirth. This great note-worthy gift, the womb, also connects you to life on the earth, the soul, and God who is the giver of life. It's from your belly and core that you seek God.

Reflection Moment: God wants you to know Him personally. In what ways can you connect to The Creator better?

~~⌒

-salvation-

Whether you believe the Bible or not, don't discount such a great book that has transformed humanity and the world. It is God's inspired Word and the most accurate and copied book ever. The Bible should not be taken out of consideration as it is God's chosen way to reveal Himself and His plan of salvation. This written form has touched lives of the past, present, and will continue onto succeeding generations. The Bible is a way that we may know and *fellowship* fellowship with God. The Bible provides records of God's grace and forbearance, interpreting warnings and renewed promises of grace for the future.

Although you cannot completely understand or define God, the Bible allows you to discover more about His nature and character providing further insight into who God is. There are four descriptions...

God is Spirit not a physical being and because of that Israel could not make any images of Him.

God is light referencing to the glory and majesty of God. In God there is no darkness (1 John 1:5). He is a sovereign God (1 Tim. 6:15,16).

God is love encompassing grace, kindness, and mercy. When we dwell in love, we dwell in God (1 John 4:16).

God is a consuming fire which refers to the holiness and complete righteousness of God's nature. Fire is frequently used as a symbol of God and His judgment against sin.

Seek to understand God's perspective to gain the larger view of self, the world, and purpose

The gift of salvation is received based on your faith in Christ and His grace. God's Spirit in your life assures you that you are His (Rom. 8:16). And the work of God's Spirit is comforting. In 1 Corinthians 2:15 it says, "But he that is spiritual judgeth all things, yet he himself is judged of no man." The Spirit provides an empowering perspective of life. This cannot be achieved or sustained by ourselves. Only God provides spiritual wisdom, spiritual guidance, spiritual transformation, and spiritual gifts. The Spirit offers freedom from the law *freedom* of sin and death that's promised to those who accept God. Scripture says that the Spirit and the Bride (church) will be issued an invitation for all who are thirsty to come and drink of the water of life (Rev. 22:17). A journey, with clarity, begins with a spiritual connection that takes you closer to the larger picture of purpose.

Reflection Moment: Choices define your understanding (discipline, thoughts, emotions, social relations, soul, etc) of yourself. Is your life reflecting your understanding?

-divine inspiration-

Inspiration derives from the Latin word in spiro meaning "to breathe in". It's said that inspiration is what artists use as the force moving the brush to many of the world's most priceless portrait(s). God breathes inspiration into your identity and direction to reveal truth that you could not otherwise comprehend. This falls into the category of a revelation, which is an uncovering, removal of the veil, or disclosure of what was not previously known; a manifestation. In this way, you know and fellowship with God bridging the connection between The Creator and creation. Finally, remember your spiritual *foundation* foundation is the most intimate part of your being. It supports, forms, and arranges all preceding layers. The spirit separates you from inorganic objects or dead organisms. Therefore, when you put the health of your spirit first, the soul and body naturally align correctly. The spirit (breath) keeps you truly alive and therefore should a priority. Remember, God will preserve, refresh, and restore your spirit. He will empower you to accomplish every task set before you. Remain spiritually sensitive, which is an awareness or knowledge of your spiritual needs bringing them to the forefront of your whole being. Be led by the Spirit. God is constantly calling and drawing you to fellowship with Him. All you have to do is yield and receive. Your relationship with God is everything!

> Women scored higher than males in standard tests of emotion recognition, social sensitivity & empathy. Neuroimaging studies investigated these findings further & discovered that women utilize more areas of the brain containing mirror neurons than males when they process emotions.

God wants to be in every experience of
creation; governing all creation

-overcomer-

You lack nothing. It's so important that you know you have the power to accomplish everything set before you. You've been given the right and authority, by God, to rule over the earth with power and dignity. In order to overcome any challenge, you must *be aware* first be aware of it. In other words, you can't act like it doesn't exist.

Recognize conditions and situations that seem to deflate your self-respect, favorable impression of yourself, and confidence. Also, identify the invisible barriers that make it difficult for women to rise in the ranks, as it will help you harness the power of the truth applying it to the situation before you. Whether or not you agree the glass ceiling is still in place, slightly cracked, or even real, women continue to face challenges every day. Real pressure to conform to the male leadership model, which involves us sacrificing or giving up one or more of our inherent sources of strength. We need to lean in to building a stronger personal existence outside of the behavior patterns and general conceptions of old mindsets. It should include liberating ourselves and our daughters from restrictions not just in corporations but in the world.

I believe glass ceilings represent strongholds that keep us from walking in the freedom destined for us. They're unclear purpose, negative portrayal, abuse, and barriers attached to low self-esteem affecting our relationships, health, and career. Glass ceilings are made to be broken. We are man's counterpart, intellectual companion, and completion. We bring life spiritually, mentally, and physically. Again, seek God daily. He will lead and protect you. He will be your resting place and He will restore your soul. Remove impurities that distance you from God, restricting you're access to Him. Release detrimental things (bad habits) that restrict the spirit. Romans 12:2 tells us, "Do not conform to the pattern of this world, but be transformed by the renewing of your mind. Then you will be able to test and approve what God's will is—his good, pleasing and perfect will."

Reflection Moment: Blessed is she who has believed that the Lord would fulfill His promises to her (Luke 1:45). What promises has God made to you?

9 781662 861321